CW01661690

NEW AND CO

Jeffrey Wainwright was born in Stoke-on-Trent in 1944 and was educated locally and at the University of Leeds. He has taught at the University of Wales, Long Island University in Brooklyn and for many years at the Manchester Metropolitan University where he was Professor in the Department of English and its Writing School until 2008.

To Judith
and in memory of my mother and father

JEFFREY WAINWRIGHT

NEW & COLLECTED POEMS

CARCANET POETRY

First published in Great Britain in 2026 by
Carcanet
Main Library, The University of Manchester
Oxford Road, Manchester, M13 9PP
www.carcanet.co.uk

A CIP catalogue record for this book is available from the British Library.

ISBN 978 1 80017 565 5

Book design by Andrew Latimer, Carcanet
Typesetting by LiteBook Prepress Services
Printed in Great Britain by SRP Ltd, Exeter, Devon

MIX
Paper | Supporting responsible forestry
FSC® C014540
www.fsc.org

The publisher acknowledges financial assistance from Arts Council England.

Supported using public funding by
ARTS COUNCIL ENGLAND

CONTENTS

Heart's Desire (1978)

Selected Poems (1985)

The Red-Headed Pupil (1994)

Out of the Air (1999)

Clarity or Death! (2008)

The Reasoner (2012)

What Must Happen (2016)

As Best We Can (2020)

Here on Earth (2022)

New Poems

I

1978

I / *The Mill-Girl*

Above her face
Dead roach stare vertically
Out of the canal.
Water fills her ears,
Her nose her open mouth.
Surfacing, her bloodless fingers
Nudge the drying gills.

The graves have not
A foot's width between them.
Apprentices, jiggers, spinners
Fill them straight from work,
Common as smoke.

Waterloo is all the rage;
Coal and iron and wool
Have supplied the English miracle.

II / *Another Part of the Field*

The dead on all sides –
The fallen –
The deep-chested rosy ploughboys
Swell out of their uniforms.

The apple trees,
That were dressed overall,
Lie stripped about their heads.

'The French cavalry
Came up very well my lord.'
'Yes.   And they went down
Very well too.
Overturned like turtles.
Our muskets were obliged
To their white bellies.'

No flies on Wellington.
His spruce wit sits straight
In the saddle, jogging by.

III / *The Important Man*

Bothered by his wife
From a good dinner,
The lock-keeper goes down
To his ponderous water's edge
To steer in the new corpse.

A bargee, shouting to be let through,
Stumps over the bulging lengths
Of his hatches,
Cursing the slowness
Of water.

The lock-keeper bends and pulls her out
With his bare hands.
Her white eyes, rolled upwards,
Just stare.

He is an important man now.
He turns to his charge:
The water flows uphill.

IV / *Death of the Mill-Owner*

Shaking the black earth
From a root of potatoes,
The gardener walks
To the kitchen door.

The trees rattle
Their empty branches together.

Upstairs the old man
Is surprised.
His fat body clenches –
Mortified
At what is happening.

THE GARDEN MASTER

The gardener digs his trench for planting.
He uses stakes and old string for his line,
A riddle to take stones from his best soil.

His master pokes around, inquires,
Points with his stick but dare not interfere.
Later he finds his shears rusting in the long grass.

The redcurrant bushes should be moved today.
The hedges are only half-finished
And privet left lying will poison the soil.

But the gardener talks to a man
By the bottom gate, then leaves.
The master is able only to let it happen.

Several days pass by the untended garden.
The cook has to come out herself
To search for cabbages among the weeds.

The master, increasingly outraged,
Fumes after that neglectful gardener
And is expected to act soon.

Who was it last lived at the ruined cottage?
In your story the gardener met the miner,
Sat out the night, and did not go home.

No one saw hide nor hair of them again.
At length the furniture was removed –
Some sold in lots, some given away, some burnt.

Behind his walls, glass set in the top,
Behind his rows of trees, his rain,
His long garden now in rack and ruin,

The master lies, as though himself
Starched into his sheets, dying,
Though as he believes, only wintering.

THE MIGRANT FROM ENGLAND

A rusty sign and tire tracks
E – Z OFF   E – Z ON

He has a limp now and a scar
and his teeth are plugged

What do you do where nothing grows,
sell cigarettes?

Nope. Beer and whiskey
if your money's good
just beer and whiskey.

*

When my wife left
I had just my two sons –
my gospel children.

One of them walked out
when he was sixteen
– never a word –
and came back

six years later.
Hullo Dad he said
… I threw him out.

The other still lives
to the north of here
and calls on holidays.
He has no sons and no wife.

*

I knew a man once who'd say

Praise the Lord who will help Man
Make a Paradise of this Earth!

'It's possible, you know,' he used to say,
'It's possible.'

*

when death shall close mine eyes

I saw a book in a store once
a picture of an old Indian in it
left by all his tribe in a cave
or some hole in the rock

I'm no Indian
shouldn't have to end up that way
in this shack, a filling station,
or any other damn place.

*

In deserts, they say the Sun is Hell
And the Moon is Paradise,
And that's the way I've found it.

That sign lights up at night for Rheingold
And it's more than a rush candle to me
Coming back from a piss in the dark.

I'm looking westward
'cause that's where the sun sets
Down and a-cries to hisself.

SENTIMENTAL EDUCATION

Delicatesse

Word of this 'revolution' drifts to us.
I sit, smoke, pore over papers
For the experts' views–though you distract me.
One can conjure whole suburbs, postmen,
Plumbers, flushed inelegant shopgirls
Ardent to be tearing up cobble stones.

What is all that compared with an eel stew,
Chicken, hard bread, and wine sharp on the tongue?
We eat ravenously, honest jagged knives
In our hands, the light of candles
Surrendering to your eyes. Ah my sweet,
To lose you will be such delicious sorrow!

The Ruin'd Abbey

A thousand years ago, the monks hereabouts
Would recognize early promise. There were
Openings for the right humility,
The sound contribution to scholarship.
Founded on such rock, juggler or jongleur,
There was no need to play with words.

I see you are not interested.
But where you sit to take off your shoes
Are tiles beautifully engraved with the Serpent
And the Fruit. Aware as I am of my own
Glibnesses, repetitions, minor faults, it is
A theme I never cease to contemplate.

The Forest of Fontainebleau

We admire the woodmen standing as we pass.
They sulk handsomely from the shoulders
Like beasts of the dark trees, wary of us.
One of them moves forward, and from a box,
Deliberately, staring straight into our eyes,
Produces three adders posed in his hands.

God knows it I am with you! all your trials
And your vexations and how you weigh them here
Bear upon me. But these your lithe spokesmen are
Too salutary, too quick. Show them to
Students, the educated poor, and tourists
Looking for something to amuse their friends.

THE SILVER EAGLE

Map tables of veined marble; state rooms; desks; clerks.
The Secretary of State comes in at three.
It is November: his aide puts on the lights,
Rinses his cup and saucer and lays them out.

War is to be detested for its savagery.
If cannons boom once more in the Medway towns
Think of the domestic misery that will ensue.
But men are happy; the brute world soluble.

A silver eagle perched on Wilhelm's beaver

A silver eagle melted from an inkstand

Shrieks

'No, that is not true!
I warn you that is not true!'

THREE POEMS ON THE BATTLE OF JUTLAND 1916

'After that we sent up shells with a message of hate…
I could not sleep for the memory of the sights I saw that day…'

I / *H.M.S. Invincible*

Shoals of North Sea cod
Are interrupted by an Admiral
Swallowing their live water.
He dies screaming
In broad fathoms among
Coal shovels and scalded stokers
Suddenly washed of their dust.

The scrupulous historian tells
Of six survivors. One thousand
And twenty-one went
Scrambling down. The facade
Invincible, bow and stern,
Subsides: two hulks.

II / *H.M.S. Black Prince*

As night came,
the cruiser Black Prince,
steaming trustily in pursuit,
fell in with
the German fleet,
thinking them British.

The Germans, guilty of
no such error,
turned efficiently
to send her down.

Some of the men
floated for a while,
shouting to each other
among chewed boats and comrades.
None was saved.

III / *Summary*

A padre rescues a parrot
From plucked extinction.

Fisher shifts for his grave
But his dream just holds.

Brisk gunners, unhooded now,
Turn in their bunks with open eyes.

The sea resumes impatiently
Its measured swell.

Both sides claim victory.

THE WAR WITH JAPAN

i.m. Percy Whiston, died 1944.

In that last evening the hot glazed sea
By Java rocked then stilled, smoothing itself.
Luckless, sick of the prison ship, and un-
serviceable as he now was, the boy died.

The sea rocked then stilled. Slowly he turned, as
Though in a hand, a figure gilding and
Decorating itself. He was consumed
There – all his life and loves – *'Abide with me!'*

BEFORE BATTLE

Our precious earth has borne us on her breast all night.
We rise and leave her, embrace each lovely comrade,
And descend, like reapers to the battle place.

The cries that come and so break up the air dissolve.
Tomorrow dances on a field of peace,
Phlox, carnation, chamomile.
We wade so deep in our desire for good.

II

THOMAS MÜNTZER

for David Spooner

Thomas Müntzer was a Protestant reformer in the early years of the German Reformation. He was a radical and a visionary both in theology and politics for whom religious thought and experience became integrated with ideas and movements towards social revolution.

Travelling through Germany, preaching and writing, continually in trouble with the authorities, he came to support and lead struggles by common people against the monopolies of wealth and learning. In 1525, in the Peasant War, he led an army against the princes which was heavily defeated at Frankenhausen. Müntzer was subsequently captured and executed.

Doubt is the Water, the movement
to good and evil. Who swims on the
water without a saviour is between
life and death –Müntzer

I have seen in my solitude
very clear things
that are not true. –Machado

I.

Just above where my house sits on the slope
Is a pond, a lodge when the mine was here,
Now motionless, secretive, hung in weeds.

Sometimes on clear nights I spread my arms wide
And can fly, stiff but perfect, down
Over this pond just an inch above the surface.

When I land I have just one, two drops of water
On my beard. I am surprised how quick
I have become a flier, a walker on air.

II.

I see my brother crawling in the woods
To gather snails' shells. *This is not*
A vision. Look carefully and you can tell

How he is caught in the roots of a tree
Whose long branches spread upwards bearing as
Fruit gardeners and journeymen, merchants

And lawyers, jewellers and bishops,
Cardinals chamberlains nobles princes
Branch by branch kings pope and emperor.

III.

I feel the very earth is against me.
Night after night she turns in my sleep
And litters my fields with stones.

I lie out all summer spread like a coat
Over the earth one night after another
Waiting to catch her. And then

She is mine and the rowan blooms –
His black roots swim out and dive to subdue her –
His red blood cracks in the air and saves me.

IV.

How many days did I search in my books
For such power, crouched like a bird under
My roof and lost to the world?

Scholars say God no longer speaks with' us
Men – as though he has grown dumb, lost his tongue,
(Cut out for stealing a hare or a fish?)

Now I explode – out of this narrow house,
My mind lips hands skin my whole body
Cursing them for their flesh and their learning –

V.

dran dran dran we have the sword–the purity
Of metal – the beauty of blood falling.
Spilt it is refreshed, it freshens also

The soil which when we turn it will become
Paradise for us once rid of these maggots
And their blind issue. They will seek about

And beg you: 'Why is this happening to us?
Forgive us Forgive us', pleading now for
Mercy a new sweet thing they've found a taste for.

VI.

So you see from this how I am – Müntzer:
'O bloodthirsty man' breathing not air
But fire and slaughter, a true phantasist –

'A man born for heresy and schism',
'This most lying of men', 'a mad dog'.
And all because I speak and say: God made

All men free with His own blood shed.
Hold everything in common. Share evil.
And I find I am a god, like all men.

VII.

He teaches the gardener from his trees
And the fisherman from his catch, even
The goldsmith from the testing of his gold.

In the pond the cold thick water clothes me.
I live with the timorous snipe, beetles
And skaters, the pike smiles and moves with me.

We hold it in common without jealousy.
Touch your own work and the simple world.
In these unread creatures sings the real gospel.

VIII.

I have two guilders for a whole winter.
I ask for company and food from beggars,
The very poorest, those I fancy most

Blessed… I am in love with a girl
And dare not tell her so… she makes me
Like a boy again – sick and dry-mouthed.

How often have I told you God comes only
In your apparent abandonment. This is
The misery of my exile – I was elected to it.

IX.

My son will not sleep. The noise
And every moving part of the world
Shuttles round him, making him regard it,

Giving him – only four years old! – no peace.
He moves quietly in his own purposes
Yet stays joyless. There is no joy to be had,

And he knows that and is resigned to it.
At his baptism we dressed him in white
And gave him salt as a symbol of this wisdom.

X.

I am white and broken. I can hardly gasp out
What I want to say, which is: *I believe in God…*
At Frankenhausen His promised rainbow

Did bloom in the sky, silky and so bold
No one could mistake it. Seeing it there
I thought I could catch their bullets in my hands.

An article of faith. I was found in bed
And carried here for friendly
Interrogation. They ask me *what I believe.*

XI.

Their horsemen ride over our crops kicking
The roots from the ground. They poison wells
And throw fire down the holes where people hide.

An old woman crawls out. She is bleeding
And screaming so now they say they are sorry
And would like to bandage her. She won't

Go with them. She struggles free. *I see it*
I see it – she is bound to die…
This is the glittering night we wake in.

XII.

I lie here for a few hours yet, clothed still
In my external life, flesh I have tried
To render pure, and a scaffold of bones.

I would resign all interest in it.
To have any love for my own fingered
Body and brain is a luxury.

History, which is Eternal Life, is what
We need to celebrate. Stately tearful
Progress… you've seen how I have wept for it.

III

FIVE WINTER SONGS

Flower mornings
Of coldest winter
Remember my child
Born in the frost
Asleep in the frost

Cold December
Clear iron mornings
The sky from darkness
Pours down flowers
Made there for you

Remember my child
Bom in the frost
Arm by his face
Stretched out he sleeps
Sleeps in the frost

*

Avenue of limes
Ignore the wind
Though you need breath
Keep still if you can
Let him sleep

Surprised by dreams
He turns and rises
And walks his room

Recognise his tears
Let him sleep

Avenue of limes
Cold as sealskin
Keep still
Though we cannot save him
Let him sleep

*

When that I see
The naked child
Fall to the grave
The tangled limbs
Of others laid

When that I see
The naked child
Losing her breath
Wounds upon flesh
Their life have kept

I ought to weep
If I any love know
As our passion moves
My love if I
Any love know

*

The winter rouses
All my grief
And feeds despair

From every hand
And feeds despair

The trees in grief
Their hearts display
Grand winter takes
With every hand
Deep in the love

Of his own demand
Arrogant thief
Arrogant thief
The winter rouses
All my grief

*

The slow-worm sleeps
So blindly coiled
And blest in blindness
Lightly laid
Survives the winter deeps

The fish in cold
Preserve their flesh
Living in latch
With the river land
They wait in winter's fold

Driving across
The lifeless night
The straight road freezes
Into light
Sleep my child my winter's loss

*

HEART'S DESIRE

heart

sleep breath

desire light

dream

If all this world were mine
From the ocean to the Rhine,
I could give up its charms,
To have the Queen of England
Lie here in my arms.
Anonymous, 12th-century German

ONE LOVE POEM

after Lorca

Oh, how hard it is
for us to love each other
at all!

For this love
the air, my heart, my hat,
hurt me.

And your eyes hurt,
you walk slower,
you wait, and go on.

How hard it is
for us to love each other
as we do.

THE DAY COMES

Lain close all night:
The moon a steady breathless sail.
The coming light
Is frozen out of air.

My love says it cannot be the day –
The light must deceive –
The lark, crying in the air
It loves, lies to us.

Daylight as thin as this
I wish would never come.
We are recovered from the dark
To part and walk about again.

THE TABLEAU

We wake up into desire

A perfect tree
Light left to itself
Unruffled beasts
The sky and the earth
Embraced like friends
Us people
Clearly naked

Your slim tongue moves
Beneath my lip

Upon your handsome body
Is put the flesh
Of this desire

THE FIERCE DREAM

I dreamt last night
A fierce dream
Of a tree
That in my garden grew,
But the garden became
A burying ground,
From the graves sleek flowers drew.

The summer so
Encased the air
It seemed we moved
In a golden bell.
But all the time
From the springing tree
The leaves and blossoms fell.

The blossom I caught
In a yellow jug,
But that then slipped my hand –
Upon the flag below
A single sound.
Pearls and red drops
From all the fragments flow.

A dream so struck
From ragged sleep
Sucks out the redness
From the day.
The mind swoons to see again
How it contrives
Its own dismay.

DESPAIR (DESESPERADA)

The day its steady breath conspires…
… we are caught in it.

Worse yet the heart is its ally,
Intending good, but involved.

It is incomprehensible –
More than any of us can embrace.

'Serene will be our days and bright
And happy will our nature be
When love is an unerring light
And joy its own security.

– if it is true
a passion for phrases does
dry up the heart
what then does silence do
desesperada?

The day its steady breath conspires;
We speak the speech of love and pain.
We fight – to want our own desires –
Our dealing hearts and flying brain.

ILLUMINATION

That is her lover lying there,
And she beside him lying close.
They do not speak, or move, or touch.
The lucid grass between them flows.

To lie, in stillness, breathing just,
Might motion time towards desire.
The air now barely moves the grass.
The sun in white draws off its fire.

SOME PROPOSITIONS AND PART OF A NARRATIVE

1. History cannot be grasped in the embrace of lovers.

2. There is love, but only as a little moment in their lives. History is untouched.

3. So it must be held that what history is, is how man deals with death, how he strives for a world where, at the last, death can be acceptable to all.

4. But not knowing history as we might, we seek a human lover – for the time being – to escape ourselves alone, to overlap one with another: 'the body of me to all I meet or know'.

… as we left he said, 'Sometimes it seems to me that every thought I have suspects the last.'

A month later we saw the coachman again. He told us that one night the soldiers came back, broke their way in, and saying that he could not see anyway, took out his eyes. 'It seems,' he said, 'I don't know who to please.'

LOVE IN THE ARMS OF DEATH

Look at love in the arms of death,
So nearly won by his slender hands.
How he catches her rising breath
And robes her body where she stands.

He turns his head to weep for her
– His love is plain for all to see.
She finds within his touch a lover
Kinder than any man could be.

(★ ★ ★)

I wish for a strong heart
  As strong as sedge
Or reed or mallow grass.

I wish that this heart might
  Stare into water
And love what it sees.

The heart I want, so strong
  That it can bear
To love itself, loves you.

I

TRANSITIVE

in memory of Daniel Richardson

'The body makes love possible' – Galway Kinnell

This stripe of light
we lie inside,
a curtain crack,
carries me to you.
Another day,
a window breeze,
touching my shoulder, speaks
of what is realized,
like how you walk, or eat,
or dress, or sleep.
Love is made tenable
in skin and bone.

But if what is loved
is drawn away –
You saw the dead child
as he was given back to her.
You saw him leave
for his frozen world,
carried to its edge
in his father's arms,
the shapes of breath about him
pulled apart

and thinned
into the passing air.

Where he is
the soil stirs by him,
slanting his body
in a run of sand,
tamps him to itself,
lets go, and slides him again.
Casting above that,
the human eye seeks light
in what is shed
upon the world
and in the globe
where it resides.

So, grasped everyday
in a key-fob photograph,
or on a sideboard,
or pressed between pages,
he is immanent –
even soldered into marl
and the city's infill
he is imaginable.
What is in the mind
cannot be touched.
The lack of him
beats at the iron ground.

The stripe of light
we lie inside
carries me to you.
I can touch you,
pass from myself,

and in this accomplished
sentence: I love you.
With less – with what
is in the mind,
what is made possible
by the idea of him,
they love.

SEA DREAMS

'I have seen enough of the obedient sea wave forever lashing the obedient shore. I find no emblems here that speak any other language than the sleep and abandonment of my woods and blueberry pastures at home.' – Emerson, *Notebooks*

The sea imagines
That it loves the land
As fire loves flesh.
It draws the shingle
To itself, breath
On breath on breath.

It dreams within
Its sleepless mind
The dreams of stones
The dreams of fish,
The life of water
Dreamt away.

As fire would ravel
Flesh it comes,
This weight of dreams
Upon its back

And rages
For the folded land.

The sea imagines
That it knows its death,
And hauls it here,
The single labour
Of its mind, the loving
Burden of its breath.

*

The sea dreams
It will catch the air,
That weightless touch
Upon its back,
And draw it past
Their perfect seal.

Air leads the water
By its breath,
Hurt with its load
The staggered sea
Strives for that breath
The life above.

It waits for pause,
For the air's caress,
To bring it muffled
Through its weight
To the smothered body
Of itself.

Along their restless line
They lie,

The sleep of its death
Is the sea denied,
The joy of its life
The air forgets.

*

The dreams of the sea
Are its only life,
Flares in the cold
And wakeful deep,
Its shapeless mind
Destroys itself.

Closing its eyes,
The sea within,
The mind becomes
The sea enclosed,
Back and back
A wave in glass.

Dreaming itself
Into every breath
The smothered sea
Enfolds the mind,
The mind unshaped
Destroys itself.

Its shadows swim
Inside the sea,
The wave embraced
To its simple end,
All of its life
Is dreamt away.

*

THE SWIMMING BODY

I

In this world or out of it? –
The senses mostly muffled up for a while;
Or lapped in its elements,
Even this simple exemplary tank
Has the world's halves, and gives a line
To be followed, and followed.

I've pressed the goggles to my face,
Decided whether to jump or dive,
And now follow the line, breathing by the book,
Using the water as a pillow, rolling right
Behind the bow-wave, centreing to look
Straight in front, just below the surface,
The elbow high on entering, the hand palm down
Between shoulder and head, looking for it there,
Seeking its feel and its catch on the water
To draw movement from it.
Thinking on these things
Is enough for the mind,
Covered by this body, stretching with it
For its breath but with nothing more to do
With the world of air.

II

I am the first one there and stand looking
At the empty pool, still, bluish, and
Cleanly cut, its lines combed straight
To stay straight no matter
How the water shivers and rocks with swimmers.

The line of water and air too is still
And looks as if it would hold even if,
By an uncle's conjuring trick
The pool could be turned up,
No drop would fall to the ceiling.
To swim is to break and not break that line,
To cut it and leave it as you found it,
To love the old and simple world of water
And to need the air.

III

Imagine living in the deeps of this pool,
A silent, nearly signless world.
Imagine thinking that this is the world
You tread the surface of.
That shifting light above is somewhere else,
Maybe desirable, by turns brighter or darker,
With a shape sometimes flagging across;
But forever out of reach,
Whatever it may prove to be, – except
Once maybe, following some glint,
Neck stretched back, you kick upwards
And bob into this world.
And if you could hold the sight,

Would you recognise it as 'purer
And more beautiful', true light
Shed freely, the true and proper place?
Or not bear the fullness of what you see,
And go again, twirl slowly away
Through the dense water and its thicker
And thicker green.

Though maybe you would sink
Gratefully, and see that this is the direction
We'd wish to go, that breaking the line
To truth, to heaven, to love,

We would find that they are simplicity, nothingness,
Lines.

The tiles are sheer and meet with all their angles.
There is the blue of a good sky, or a lucent green.
It feels heavy, clothing, like a blanket;
It is quiet, and drawn over against the clamour
Carried in the shifting air.
We could live here if we could deserve it,
A simple utopia, a room cut from the ocean,
Regularised, oblong, uncomplicated,
No shadow or shade, unpocked
By inlets, creeks, seething tide-pools,
Any of the brocades and broideries of weed
That look only acted upon but are at work,
A thousand mouths, and nothing in that great
Voracity that cannot think but what it needs.
Here it is like the skull scoured out,
A white chamber, the bone shining like steel
And reflecting only itself.

IV

The mind as it lives with itself,
Noticing, taking things in, pondering,
Dismissing from its presence, allowing some things
To slip out, hit by recollection,
Looking forward (tonight, the summer),
Seems to float free, say, as I walk across
This park, just in front and a foot to the side.
Today there is a tune, some serious matter
For a while, bits of books, a meal,
An old friend in his gaberdine.
It can't keep to anything,
Its sentences are left open, it is a conversation
Of unfinished thoughts, unfinishable, but
Running, running, even as it thinks of itself
As itself, intelligence, consciousness,
'The life of the mind' – and here it might be pleased –
What else cam the soul be?

I am on my way to swim, the mind alongside
As I say, moving briskly in the cold through
Some interest or other, spending some time
On what to do – how many lengths, in what pattern?
Re-running Salnikov, today's sports page:
A 100 in under a minute times 15!
Be solicitous but stern with the lungs
And the aching arm.

The trees in the park are shuttered.
A young man comes into view, his hair shaved up
Around his ears, his shoes laceless and without socks.
He is speeding round the paths turning
In sharp angles and shrieking as he goes,

A huge, strange call like a bird
From some land of marsh and cloud.
The mind has noticed this and is
Drawing back. If I pick up my pace,
Barely noticeably, we will be carried beyond him
As he arrives at the next comer and
Twirls on the ball of his foot towards us.
The mind is back inside, to the matter in hand,
No intention of being left to face a mind
Bodied out as this is in its dented and
Bundled flesh, its tiny running steps,
Strange curvets, and the wave beat of his cry
Pushing the air towards us. What
Comes down the path here, the vast chest,
The gait, the head, the face in white,
Is his mind, a physical thing as is my own,
Shrunk back now to be in step.

As the mind comes back it is not to prison
But itself. If I am not outside my body –
A foot to the side, a foot in front –
Neither is this body merely a house,
A space, a lodging, cavity, lathboard crack,
But something that is fluent in the mind,
As the mind itself is mortised
In this body's nervousness.

What the mind makes of anything comes of how
The body's made, as through the limb of sight,
Or what it touches and what touches it,
Like this water slipping past, happening
Outside the brain but not simply arriving there
To be noticed but already having joined us
At the skin. This is the border of the world,

The edge of space, the tireless lapping
Of the thought of truth, the pulse of death,
The simple outline of the self – here, and
Here, and here – the edge inventing the idea
Of itself
Of what it is and what it might be
Of what it is and what it might be
And so on and so on and so on.
Everything comes by the body and is streaked by it.

ILLUSORY WARS... 1924... 1944... 1984

'Lord Esher delivered lectures on the lesson of *The Great Illusion* ... A twentieth century war would be on such a scale, he said, that its inevitable consequences of commercial disaster, financial ruin and individual suffering would be 'so pregnant with restraining influences' as to make war unthinkable.'

'Tears came even to the most bold and resolute.'

Barbara Tuchman, *August 1914*

1/1914

Ambassadors, generals, secretaries for war
Have done so much to get themselves so far
And they weep. In the amber of Petersburg
Emissaries embrace; Churchill crosses the kerb

On the short walk to where he will cry,
Blubber, sob, melt like Monsieur Messimy
At the same hour in tears as he comes to speak,
His mind gulped suddenly by what will break.

Their fingers trace small pebbled lanes across
Glistening fields, past gardens with some trellis
Of clematis or vine, a corner for gooseberries,
The banging of a lattice door that carries

Over the way on the quickening wind.
As they inch on from Kovno to Ostend
They brush the Channel with their braided cuffs,
Thread the nations, and pull at handkerchiefs.

II / 1944

A water-butt has us clinging to its rim.
A boys' adventure would be to tipple in
Like frogmen, sound and swim the inkwell,
And fasten our charges to the Tirpitz's hull.

The triumphal generation of small boys
Play dead, go hand to hand from house to house:
My cousin, smithereened again, yet lives;
My uncle, tipped into a distant sea, dives

From the light forever; my father
On his leave lets his uniform lie like a
Dummy where it's fallen –
Meine familie ist alles jetzt gefallen.

But warned and circumspect we take due care
Of garden terrors, stay near to the door,
Our allotment, bit of waste ground,
Nation, saved for us, the back lawn wunderkind.

III / 1984

Un and im – unimaginable, unwageable,
Unprofitable, improbable – will
Keep us calm. Perhaps the dead of those wars
Only pretend: an infantryman clambers

From the sticky field, a sapper rises
From a roadside drain, like pearl-divers
Able seamen kick back to the sun
And bob by their children in the warm lagoon.

The nations, twined across every garden plot,
Are now so interlaced, so much in one boat
Together, their hulls bumping the ice
Together, both conquered, they shall embrace.

Acid-free pages turning in the breeze,
The histories of future fiction erase
The heavy lanes and the ministers who weep.
My son reads Liquidate Paris! as he drops to sleep.

LEGAL CRIMES: THE NURSE-TREE

Human dreams, worked up in the capable mind,
Phrased into flesh, come out and perform on earth, in air,
    in time,
.... as with... this man: a handsome soul,
As evil as ourselves, silvered by imagination
To be our example, a tooth drawn
For sorcery, the token of a better age,
His light body flexed and hung
Out of the love we bear ourselves,
Love for the precious grave.

THE MAD TALK OF GEORGE III AND A HYMN TO LIBERTY

'...A century that thinks about liberation and phantasises prisons...'

Hans Magnus Enzensberger

I

The slow-worm from my orchard seeking me
Creeps to my counterpane and waits,
His body curled here in my linened hands.
I lift him up and wind him round
My temples like a tender vine
Bringing his head to rise so neatly from my brow.
He is the slender vessel of my power,
My man of justice, not the stricken silver
Of a Pharaoh's crown but moving flesh,
And able to embrace us all.

II

I sit alone in my chair on the bare moor,
The grass in flood in the orb I hold.
I sit as I did for anointment:
Attendants bringing up the coy canopy,
Archbishop Ambergris mounting the steps
To smooth my tousled head
For ministers to tell me their tales,
Doctors of the nerves, philosophers,
The black child of 'la liberté',
His eyes like scorched stones.

*

I sit alone in my chair on the bare moor,
Monarch of the yellow grass that laps my feet,
Of fearful space, a saucer of tussocks
And covert pools.
I cannot abide wildness –
Satan is the prince of open air.
His will incites the mobile grass beyond itself
And hurls the tidy song-bird round the sky.
He it is brings, bemused from his club of devils,
The black child of 'la liberté' –
The blackened child of 'la liberté' –
For me to reason with.

*

Caught in the romance of king and child,
I show the boy this man,
Put up to hang,
Dreamed out of us and labouring in the air,
Who swims for a moment, rests,
Swims, and then rests.
The earth cannot hold his stillness.

III

Candidus, my tall blood-prince, my grenadier,
Come with me since I love you.
Let us find a grove in middle Europe
Raised from sandy soil
Where the words will leave these stories
We have become and steal away,
Hallooing still one to another
Like accomplices on a dark road,
But gone.
                                        And we can dissolve,

blushes into white space   forgetting even

            the moss of a tree

                                        on its north side

the lost touch of it

A HYMN TO LIBERTY

Count all the miner's hours, all his breathing
To the point of light.

A scud of air across the water's open face;
A child dabbles the flats of her palms
And laughs as she watches their play.
Each tree its silence breaks.

The movement of a breath of air across the lips
Creates the mind, and gives all of us our lives –

The inspired Republic,
A commune like the body with the air.

The child in love with the endless lake
Draws all her breath

TO HIS LOVER

At the dead of night he breaks in upon her.

The room he knows so well,
That they have shared alike,
Is to him now the globe of his own eye
That he stumbles inside.

The bed-light flashes on and she is there,
She and some other friend, limbs thus and thus,
The sheet roped across them,
Pulled out of sleep.

– This is love he feels, something he knows he feels,
The best we can do, known to us by jealousy.

He leaves them, shoulders the laurel at the gate,
The wrought iron dragging at the paving stone,
And is back to the street,
Its heavy trees,
Pools of rigid light.

AS HE FOUND HER

She lay a long time as he found her,
Half on her side, askew, her cheek pressed to the floor.
He sat at the table there and watched,
His mind sometimes all over the place,
And then asking over and over
If she were dead: 'Are you dead, Poll, are you dead?'

For these hours, each one dressed in its figure
On the mantelpiece, love sits with him.
Habit, mutuality, sweetheartedness,
Drop through his body,
And he is not able now to touch her –
A bar of daylight, no more than
Across a table, flows between them.

THE DEAD COME BACK

The dead come back to us in dreams –
As we are told they do so they come.

Thus among the tablecloths and cakes,
The ham and sliced tongue and all the objects
Of this earth,
The company known and unknown at this latest funeral,
Lily, large and powdered in her flowery dress
Appears to her brothers and all of us
Like a star, a celebrity back among her own,
Nearly a sister again, nearly an aunt,
All of us parting for her, shy of touching
What we have brought to mind.

Unable as we are to die,
The dead come back to us in dreams –
As we are told they do, so they come.

from THE RED-HEADED PUPIL

'In vain sedate reflections we would make,
When half knowledge we must snatch, not take.'
Pope, 'Moral Essays', Epistle I

THE RED-HEADED PUPIL

Part One: The Anatomy Lesson

Prologue

Holly, how far you are from dying,
how far from ever dying! Such a head
of hair, a real bonfire flaming in the street,

happy in your skin, at least as much as
most of us could hope to be, well certainly
lucky-ish so far for nineteen years
with your trapped thumb your only lesion

or serious bump from life – admit it!
Look how the city concrete can turn rose
in the four o'clock winter sun –
Then don't – pick what you want for your mind,
things of your own to make the neurons fire!

I

In some river, any day of the week,
some figure bumps against the bridge-pile
and is left as the current passes.

One could be draped in with rags and branches,
another arched and stretched like a backstroker
starting, another sprawled on a settee,
perhaps slalom poles bob on their wires nearby.

Whoever comes there just turns up without
benefit of bread packed with mercury
and cast upon the waters: one who maybe
watched the weed-tresses combed by the stream, carried
an air-gun for rats, or just came and walked in.

II

For this bridge the firemen have a drill set.
Though the channel is wadeable to the bar,
then they are in the full, deep-cut race

so must be equipped up to spec, their skill
tallied to the job in hand so that a hoist
and a cradle-drop from the second span
can lean over and draw him from the flume.

To be re-gathered, re-numbered,
an obligation set by the hopeful
ordinance that none shall be lost in death,
that given names shall be found, and a duty done
each effaced, replaceable citizen.

III

Exact cause: something to be found, something
to be entered, a last dent that can stand
as this man's very last particular.

Imagine a wooden country room.
The township pathologist parts the skull,
perhaps handing the cap to his assistant
who holds it out like a small basin

as he unfolds the brain down either cheek,
teasing from the centre-parting of hemispheres
something that looks an impractical pink,
silly, more like an unravelled pullover
splashed with gloss and emulsion than hard-wiring.

IV

Is this where what the man is is to be found?
Is this where it all coincides, is all
gazetted, cartouched, ephemerized,

but in wisps and bobbles, not even in
circuits like the droplet solderings that sang
'It might as well rain until September',
'He's a rebel and he'll never ever be any good'?

The caretaker's small boy steals to the open door –
he wants to know what's up there but the feet
fill his view, blebbed, blistered, blained, the unique
dogs of infantry and chiropody –
'Excused boots? What makes you so different?'

V

Squeak. In a boarded nook only its own size
a mouse can hide and never pine for light,
but even so it cannot help but be.

Since everything true of a mouse and me,
as everything true of Thomas Nagel,
is already in the world – the world that is
just the world – how can we then be we

and not any of those who got off the bus
at the top of Duke Street one afternoon,
and disappeared until now, dipped deep
in the spoonable white medulla –
what is it like? How can they be them?

VI

Mad in the night with dreams ('human beings
by definition half the time mad' anyway?)
I am looking down on my own dissection.

Not Vesalius completing his book,
nor Doctor Tulp showing with his scissors' tip
how the tendons of the open forearm lie
and how the annular ligament

keeps all of them in place, could look on this
more disinterestedly than I myself –
certainly not the red-headed pupil
who looks perplexed as though the stripped-out arm
has already waved his mind elsewhere.

VII

My chest is sprung open, all abdominal
muscle and cartilage sheared away
and under the sternum where the heart

and the blue lungs lived is now a cave
a small cat could climb in. Down there, or up here
one of us ought to be scared – squeamishness
arrives routinely at even the sight

of a punctured thumb and this must be the worst
that could ever happen. But none of it hurts,
no damage is done, it is just interesting.
We are free of each other and free:
just as we always thought, we do not die.

VIII

Mad in the night with dreams… Suitcases packed,
everything we own, including blankets,
crowding the bay of somebody's front-room,

and I see over the backs where I played
and the haulage-yard of still-wet
shiny Fodens, swans crossing the sky
over Normacot, and then, very low,

a stubby airliner, much like Richard Scarry
would draw and call 'Mirabelle',
hanging upside down tethered by cables
and rigging which people are fleeing down
while others fall on daisy blooms of parachutes.

IX

Some do escape, but then the crash is real.
It is down on Buccleuch or Furness Road
and I am caught too close to do nothing.

I pick up the suitcases – all those blankets –
and set off, showing myself how
properly eager I am, but with the hope
that I will walk and walk and be too late.

Yet nothing that comes to my eyes is,
after all, insupportable. All is earth,
muddied figures, plasticine men, obscure.
Beyond the tape the crater is too deep to see.
I carry my suitcases here then there.

X

Is that how the brain makes itself useful,
toiling while we sleep, like an engine-driver,
a nightwatchman with his box and brazier,

a fluffer gathering hair from the Tube rails,
evolving something else to be good at besides
the calculation of what's too hot or too heavy?
Must be a good part of what it's fit for.

Doctor Tulp, like the best of barbers, shoots
his cuffs and begins. He combs out the axons
and dendrites, the woven feltwork of us,
and touches – does he? – the man who husks and counts
onion-skins, then… a face like a pollard knot?

XI

Or are they, to Physics, the same kind of thing
as the soul, or a haircut? Observe what
we can; instance: the annular ligament.

Seven gather round Tulp to study it.
One is fixed on the master, 'Look, I'm listening',
the next looks knowingly at the book propped
by the corpse's feet, two are intent,

one relishing this, another checking his notes,
the sixth poses, the seventh is the red-headed pupil.
Close your fist. From their condyle, flexor muscles
travel the hairy side of the arm and cock
the wrist as well. We do that without thought.

XII

Because, said George B. Bridgman, the body is
a machine. For fifty years he drew it and taught
that the fixed law of muscle is to contract

towards its centre, and all the body's cords,
pulleys, levers, declutch accordingly.
So he strips the masseter to a hinge
that lets the head's one moving bone mill

its meal and oil; he draws as a trapeze
the muscle across the shoulders that keeps
the head erect; the back as hewn planes
and a fantail of cables wedged down
into the sacrum, the body's axis,

XIII

the free fulcrum on which it turns and flees.
The foot, he says, is the envy of bridge-builders:
its keystone astralagus is not fixed

as in masonry, but floats the weight
of the whole body between the heel
and the toes as it descends step by step
to the ground where it rocks, lifts and leaves.

And wherever two bones meet, the cartilage tip
takes up the jarr on a surface smooth as cellophane,
filmed by an oil, a tiny pressing of cells
'That supples, lubricates and keeps in play
The various movements of this nice machine.'

XIV

We do all of this without thought. Stop. All this
is done without thought. Because we are
a machine – because there is a machine,

like there is a wall abutting this street,
26 feet wide, a 1910, 3-
storey gable-end, 112 flights
though by now not one brick is the same shade and feel

as another. Thus, four-square as it is,
Halifax and Leeds permanent as it is,
without new downpipes or the way soot
has filtered outwards, it must be counted
but semi-invariant since every hour the light changes it.

XV

It is almost as particular as flesh,
and brick for brick, grain for grain, hair for hair
it is the same stuff, the same compo as us.

Examine one drop of water dried into the lime:
there is still a lake-bed upturned to view;
enter one fissure, abseil to its last
unsustainable point and new caverns fall open.

At this ground, whatever wattle the mind,
whatever surprise or animation,
whatever joke splutters and laughs to itself,
'*this loam, this roughcast and this stone does show*
that I am that same wall; the truth is so.'

XVI

'*Would you desire lime and hair to speak better?*'
No, but on some days to fade into it,
which I cannot do, '*O sweet and lovely wall*'.

We are after all too different.
Nobody walks into a wall, nor runs
through it – it *is* seen, even though, full on,
some of the bricks are known to be guessed at

from their neighbours as orange patched with grey –
again an extrapolation achieved
without thought. But it is up here, on the screen,
now, with some yellow flowers, more variant,
all information for area 17.

XVII

What do I see here? *I* sees nothing.
The machine works, the piece of work that bumps
against the bridge-pile works, and that is all.

I is the body's dream, what it makes up
as it goes along. The brain cranks I out
inadvertently as it feels thirsty
and puts the kettle on – one scope and a bit.

Forget homunculus, be he Happy,
Grumpy, Bashful, Dopey, Sleepy, Doc;
forget 'I spy', forget 'Up periscope!',
the earnest youth, the boy of feeling,
forget any soul behind the night-sight.

XVIII

Up in 17 the wall is projected sunny;
next door it is warm; a metal hanger
tings like a tuning fork. Sweet somatics,

how you develop to no purpose save
to be that bit better at it next time.
Individuals strive to increase
the representation of their genes

and that is all. Organisms adapt and
that is all. Matter is the ground: mind, God,
spirit, soul arc words – lemony lichens –
workable static in the cellular
circuit boards, success.[10]

XIX

Put a picture of the brain in your mind's eye.
Done? That's not the way it is. However
dispassionate you are, you are making it up.

That very wall is not the wall you see,
not even the one the cyclist wobbled into;
the sun is not what's felt on the freckled arm;
the coathanger is not the noise it makes.

But they're not what's awkward. The brain is un-apt.
The mollusc Nautilus fills its rough eye
with sea-water and never learned to grow
even the mucoid lens of cousin squid
to give it more than a shadow of light.

XX

Into our same kind of cup the light pours
abundantly, is marshalled to needlepoint
and still the brain fumbles grey into black.

And so the lofty real can squire it forever:
unfelt gravities on the sun, sounds a dog
cannot hear, the slight secretive jostle
of particles in the unnameable wall.

Mass, shape, motion how mighty you are!
How centreless, featureless, how bleached
innocent of purpose, how little fussed!
You are the lordly nothing that is. You can
deliver us from ourselves. And that is all.

XXI

– poppy-headed, face down in the pharmacist's drawer –
Bertrand de Born swinging his own head by the hair
like a lantern crying *'Oh me!'* – mind waved aside –

not that being there in that allotment,
surrounded by the neat black soil was strange,
but that suddenly it was strange being anywhere.
So be nowhere – *'with that hair you're the one'll*

stick out, you're not mousey like the rest of them.'
One millet grain of notice blown to you
across the floor should be sufficient.
In the womb neurons die to perfect their brain
then all these bits stipple it as your own. Oh me!

XXII

Old ladies love strange flowers and their Latin names –
even in mid-winter they go to the Alpine
Garden to visit them and shuffle the snow aside.

From the cindered path and tidy soil step back –
'Contemplate Nature in her full grand majesty.'
Sca-rey. The infinite and nothing. What
each of us is compared with all that existence.

From the landau of Significance what
can be seen of us, or of neat tabs in felt-tip
tucked in the soil? But if we are nothing
so is the distance from us no more
than the thumb that brushes clear the flower's name.

XXIII

The red-headed pupil is worried he is
not following. Now he's let his mind go
to the sudden sweet crust of a bread-cake.

He tries harder. Tulp quotes Eucalyptus:
'The search for reality is as momentous
as the search for God.' And as difficult.
And perhaps the same thing. In there, minus

its life-blood, is the cadaver's mind; in
the cat's cave of his chest his heart; sticking out
his gawky feet – all planetary stuff,
including, even though evaporated now,
'What makes you so different?' 'Me feet, sarge, me feet.'

Part Two: Free Rein

I

Ecce our Jack ski-ing in the Lebanon.
Look at the smile on his face, pleased as Punch,
and just like the Aly Khan in those sunglasses.

He never did it again after the war,
but did smile truly through forty years
an insurance man – ledger, comptometer,
spreadsheet – a fine filament of it all.

The transports dot the screen above Aleppo,
levering south in wireless range of where Cain
slew Abel, and, not knowing what to do
with him, bore him on his back for forty years,
a private lifetime: brother, aircraftman.

II

Ecce the thumps and transactions of Empire:
the trowel-taps of Marduk's bricklayers,
the panel-beaters of Abilene,

the mollusc searched for its purple,
the Druze to market for his Yorkshire worsted,
the Roman miles of water carried as gently
as in a cup so the warm fig will swell,

confectionery saved for Tamburlaine in snow,
the cumulus of all things nice that made
Zenobia Queen of Arabia for a while,
wordperfect Macaulay, the Lady of Battles
with her lionhearts – Ishtar Regina.

III

And the dry-docks of Tyre, and the pepper roads
where styles of diplomacy could be pressed
and Phoenicians write their bills of sale

in letters that would spider this far
so cenotaphs can speak the names they know,
the 10000 souls under their revets of sand,
the dry mold from which the warrior is cast.

To resist Assyria, Ishtar astride her lion,
arrayed in terror, a star in her hair…
… 700 chariots… 10000 foot…
walking to the railway to the war;
simply put: nude sword to naked abdomen.

IV

To resist Assyria (Ishtar upon her lion)
a democratic vista:
Nell and Perce and Gladys and Jack:

the we the people who are the *matériel*,
the hands between the biscuit and the glaze
colouring cornflowers fifteen to the dozen
or banding Etruscanware for table and sideboard,

and saffruck, the fitters and the clerks,
the servers of school dinners,
the spotters of paths in the sky, dust clouds
in the desert, the dead of the prison-ship,
Nell and Perce and Gladys and Jack.

[after Emyr Humphreys]

V

Suppose, consider, behold, sec, know
these four and all those who for any hour
of these fifty thousand years have been a part –

dying in muffled labour for the species,
dreaming of the evening and a game of bowls,
deciding... What is it I ask you find
to do with them, and how, and why?

Only… think… Think of the number, and that
however hurried on their way, none was a speck,
a bit of all there is, of 'what happens',
not the poorest he and she of them but had
and has a life to live. Think of yourself.

VI

Once plumbed in as philosophy, that ancient rage
must now be able to describe not only
what we need but what we expect to be.

The newest child, underwater in a warm pool,
grinning and knowing from its body
how to turn and breathe without a thought,
and the silken light and the fields of morn.

And press on, beyond what it is like to be,
to the moment we can truly cry
'This is freedom, here is liberty!
This is what the foot does when the shackle's struck.'
'And down that long dark lode he skated home':

VII

Free of the march for water with an Esso can;
Free of a pop belly and grass rubbed into dust;
Free of prizing a yard of plastic as riches;

Free of gutrot, revenges, falling and sleeping;
Free of him who is exactly stronger,
the boy in judgement killing for beers and Marlboros;
Free of the bridewell and the fortress of angels;

Free of the correct listener and all nuance;
Free of skin, free of hair, of elocution, being tallest;
Free of love received and owed even past death;
Free of all believing, given or sought after;
Free to understand everything, to be beyond and nothing.

VIII

A long draught he took, and again drank deep,
into the rose-girt cistern plunged his face,
bathed in running water, as is the law.

Here on four inches of map from Punjab to the Atlas
are all the palm groves known – for five millennia
all the slow, slow bedding-in of humankind
in towns lost but alive on the 'waterless sea'.

Praise be then to every pipe-layer in his ditch,
to the stolid inspector with his wooden wand,
the Sanitary Idea and all the Chamberlains
and Averys who took the Water Works –
life and death, not source for profit – for their Birminghams.

IX

‘Hunger,’ said the poet, ‘I can bind here
in my own entrails as tight as that most
dextrous of girls can wind a thread.’

Making it something else, docs he live on fresh air?
Yet it is said the Prophet himself left this life
without feasting once on barley bread –
white flour and buttered cakes were dreams.

By tightened guts then are we come,
with – the system of account will show –
just enough calorized into the arrowhead
or we would be quite gone into the shale
and our reaching hand never drawn to world attention.

X

I’ll cat anything – only cornflakes for a week
when I have to, crisps, custard creams (3p for 2),
grass, starlings, shrews, mice, dog, suck the eyes

from a rat, or an enemy, or those
we did not need, or a hyena itself lined
with carrion, or grains I would not have bruised,
or pekelhareng or pappadelle con sugo pomodoro

or blinis or latkes or pagan spice Satanic sugar
aubergines in the lake-palace style
the fearsome pineapple bacon and cheese
with oatcakes pikelets black pudding blood
of anything to get by and get by we have.

XI

We've changed it from number 4 to 'Woodford House'.
The wife's done the lettering – she's qualified in that
and always wanted to get back to it.

I did the forecourt to get the van off the avenue
and the hardcore under there's better than the M6 –
you should see their rubbish and weep –
I bevelled the kerb so there's no Council come-back.

Mother would cry if she could see it all.
'Lived in a chimney, us,' she'd say. She gave us
this, framed: '*Who loves not home however poor? I*
Himself the master of the door.' I nearly called this
'The Poorhouse' as a sort of a joke for round here.

XII

It would be. Of all those in the queue that day
who came to breathe in and hold it and go off again
the shadow stole into the glass for me.

We do not die as much as once we did,
25 per thousand, then 15, and lower,
because of what we got to eat, because
of windows, because of drains and streptomycin.

Into the cold glass as it is slotted to and fro
as I stand hands on hips and hold my breath steals
not *tubercle bacillus* isolated, but a fear
of deserving, a caution set there forever.
What ails me is what I call a shadow.

XIII

From a little German court that could not keep itself
in firewood, to all the Russias of secret prisoners,
imperial house-dogs tried and hanged for treason,

the Empress Catherine rose from snow,
oak-leaves in her hat, a brain in her head
and government felt as a romance, a science,
silver money, no more bits of wood and marten-pelt.

'But the world I found and which we tread,' she said,
'is not an alphabet. Dream it into paradise,
dream it out of all meaning, it was never better
than this, it will never be better than this.
We do not climb the skies, we work on human skin.'

XIV

When I was young and cruel, not Tamburlaine
paddling in human blood, nor yet a true compiler
of human heads as by the road to Nanking,

but pettily, as and when I could, tormenting
the Bible-puncher in the bogs, practising
the reasons why it was all right to do this to him –
all the reasons truly were I could.

So I take my place in the back of the van,
or the gauntlet and don't know what I am,
though if it turns out what I do I'd better not,
or am found out and brought up face to face,
I know I can forget who I ever was.

XV

First off, the hangman couldn't be found no place.
I'd seen him linkin' on out of it
when he saw it comin', but he didn't let on none.

I wished he had though when ole Put turns to me
and says 'Got yourself a new job, Ginge',
and he gets Jones to climb this ladder.
I'm feeling leaky and can't get the necktie fixed.

'Sir,' says Put, 'mend your soul, step off there
and meet your Maker.' Jones don't move a flicker,
just stares out in front. Ole Put gets mad as mad,
skips around and tells me to haul that ladder away.
'No,' I says, 'I ain't goin' to do that.'

XVI

And I dragged the ladder away. When I looked,
Jones's neck was all raw and chicken-stretched,
his legs kicking the last fathom like a clam-diver.

I covered up his face, all black, one eye
clear out on his cheek, and that was so smooth
'cos he'd shaved real careful that morning
as I was standing by him holding the bowl.

And he says to me, There ain't no day
not worth shavin' for,' and he winks as he says it.
And I'm glad I remember him as he said that,
and that bowl, 'cos it done me powerful harm
to see what it was I saw that day.

[Homage to S.L. Clemens]

XVII

I am the voice that has been listening all this while,
noted precisely how it is you cannot see
there is no way the subject might be free.

Interrogate, for instance, why you like éclairs.
How was the taste constructed in your mouth?
Was it the lavishment of Mother's 'love',
that old *voyage éclair* the Culture specifies?

The way you wear your hat, especially kiss,
(*monotone et sans éclair*) there are no words
you can control, no blinding *éclairciss-*
ement available to you, I know,
no thundrous no, so – *Vous avez choisi?*

XVIII

That I, a *pícaro*, should fall in love!
And with a slave, a natural slave, a girl
who if she could care would care only for coin.

Nor did I ever take much thought for love,
nor, running low to ground, for honour neither,
not looking for a Helen boasting of gods
on both sides, but never dreaming of a slave,

of finding myself in hiding at the corner,
gawping like a Capuchin when the blacks
celebrate Our Lady of the Snows in dress
barbarous enough to guess their nakedness,
bound to a slave, for her slight limbs shamed.

XIX

The moss-rose and *The Moss-Rose*, red brick
and the redder tree wigged like a dame –
Nell and Perce and Gladys and Jack, father

lifted away. I am in a taxi with the old man
travelling up the hill, the town behind dark,
the road beyond *The Moss-Rose* moorland black,
for a sleeping moment he is back, then gone.

I go to meet my own son by my own route
and am lost in the crescents and walks,
tangled in roadworks-tape, gravel and asphalt piles.
I see him on the walkway, and behind the windscreen
cry, not weep, mouth stretched out and down.

XX

As by Random and Pickle and Clinker, spellbound:
an incident that cooled – out of hot water,
bacteria, mica: leaf and flesh – at length a wet

or a dry ape, up from the swamp or down from the trees,
hands for tools, thus mouth for speech (for the not-here,
more later) – for the brain words need: a wide pelvis,
and thus standing is also easy – so onward now,

with culture borne on women's shoulders to make the leaf
grow here and water flow there – a stone roof, a column
and lo, laws and sonnets, and then Steam
who was an Englishman, and Silicon who is not –
like that, like that, like that it was, just like that.

XXI

How beautiful are causes! the sway towards, the click,
the this because of that, the syntax
of predictive power advancing on boiling point.

Yet how we must despise them, hate them
for their fewness, for not demonstrating why
we are unquiet, for being fashioned by us
and so unable just to be themselves.

Yet wish we could descend by them, by degrees,
passing *tubercle bacillus* naked on its slide,
alighting at last in that perfect cold
where every atom stops its shuddering
save the will to know what fact will save her.

XXII

Not that. Not that. Not that. Not that. But I
am still thinking theref… Though I'd rather be –
as who would not? – nicely fat, really comfy

in winceyette, snug as a bug in a rug. And but
for some tremor or other we could be in the coverlets
of shale, the same bits of what is not, of whatever is
hiccupping through its great extinctions,

but without the t-t-t-ting of Telos – spielos Telos,
forget we ever thought of you, out of sight
out of… ah hah! nothing to believe with
and thus free as… stop it… just free as…
living as though [] don't exist. Dream on.

XXIII

In the evening, paddling pools glimpsed from a train;
a yellow squash full of the leaning sun;
a life, a very liveable life, we like more and more.

We all have projects for such happiness:
'For six months I was a French polisher in Newhaven
but all I wanted to do was sing in a band
and the world co-operated and I do.'

'He raped my daughter (12). I picked him up
from prison and took him back. Why did I?
It wasn't me. If you stand back and look at it
you'd see everything's like that, we're pushed,
and what you think is, it doesn't matter, this.

XXIV

'Then again something won't go away –
something, I can't tell what, but it says
I'm not as numb as that tree and don't want to be.'

Pouf! the Empire falls out of mind as she speaks.
Pouf! the boy kisses his captor's face.
Pouf! the old soldier spits out his plug.
'Don't want to be. Don't want to be. Don't want to be.'

A dream is not freedom but it freely comes.
It says: 'Your mind walked up here,
granite and schist underfoot, and is now
what you have become. It invented freedom
as it came, make of it what you can or will.'

THE WEAK SPOT

As if getting by,
doing a job,
roadworks, credit cards
the kid in 3 Windsor
who spits at your back,
watching and loving
your own kids
is not enough –

A swatch of her blood
drops on the tablecloth,
beads and sizzles
on the hotplates
of nan bread and dansak
as she gropes
with a napkin
to mop her nose
split and skee-wiff
– and this in public!
friends around, jumping up,
one crashing across
the table, some of them
in tears,
and it's not something
even the waiters see
too often –
who's going to sort it?
get this guy out?
And what kind of a man
does that?
The heel of his hand

back-handed
though there are
plenty to say
she's mad as an axe
has studied burglary
maybe murder
figuring out ways
to get even
wreck his place
rip up all those books
most of them
the same as she has
Viragos Paladins Vikings
The Condition of the
Working-Class in England
The Interpretation of Dreams
– all so far above
the rock and water universe
the eventual
green universe
past uninformed necessity
even the fresh red
universe of beasts –
and maybe both know
that bit of Freud
where he says about
human cultural development
and sexuality
being still
the weak spot.

Thesaurus:
377 Physical Pleasure
bodily enjoyment
gusto bonne bouche
378 Physical Pain
chafe sting bite stab.

*

Who will in
fairest book
of Nature know
how Virtue
may best lodged
in Beauty be,
let him…
  the blush of honour
the half-blown
rose

*

blossom from the car-park
tree scratches
the street –
the girls
bared and starved
as needles
greenish in the sodium
light, chlorotic,
stuff such as
a strong wind
would blow away,
first woundable

now maimed,
heroin pushed up
between the toes,
do the work
of beauty,
hanging by the wall
for john,
quids in and
bob or two john,
lickerous john,
his mind greased
to pay
and bruise for it,
peeled from
the starling swarm.

*

(from Charles Baudelaire,
'A celle qui est trop gaie')

Your head, your walk, each move of your mouth
Are like a scene in Nature
Ideally composed, the feature
That is your smile a zephyr from the south.

Any mournful man you brush by in the street
Starts, and, dazzled, steals a glance
Over his shoulder at the dance
Of your shoulder, feels its rush of heat.

When you dress, colour meets colour and halts
Amazed, each shade beating one
Upon another, taffeta silk and chiffon –
You make flowers, the poet says, waltz.

Those crazy clothes show every hue
Of what you are and each fevered part
Sets fire to some patch of my heart –
I hate you as much as adore you!

When I have got myself dressed,
Dragged myself out into the air
Of some bright garden what happens there
But the sun tears at my breast.

Springtime, greenery, the untrodden way,
All the spume of Nature's incense
Shames me to take offence,
To make one flower, one petal pay.

That's you. One night, as desire demands,
I'll come to you, slinking like a coward
Of course to your endowered
Body, and take it in my hands.

That lightsome flesh I'll then chastise.
That blameless breast prise apart,
The rib sprung back above your heart,
The gashes widening before your eyes.

And, in the vertigo of this delicious state,
Across that tender lip –
So beautiful, so sisterly – slip
The fine filtration of perfected hate.

OUT OF THE AIR

i.m. Sidney Wainwright 1910–95

Every moment is exhalation, an appointed
sacrifice, like that
poured upon the ground saying, this is what we are, no more,

thus are we expended, by reflex, just as, from that smack on,
we draw the fraction
that we need from what swathes us now

and oxidize divinity, put what should go on forever
to our use,
worked through every track and gully of this catacomb,

changed, as we perform our repetitions,
into our change,
we beings as nearly metabolous as the fly:

in the lover's lightest rise and fall asleep,
our flustered age,
within the infant's sigh a rapturous somersault.

*

Until, *de facto*, the air does not go on,
that until arrives,
– *my last breath, with my dying breath* –

and I am able to bring in no more, include,
embrace no more,
put the last roughed centilitres aside

barely drawn upon, pushed away, defrayed –
puff… puff… it goes
and there is no fellow can replace it,

and I am what I was, untouched, unentered,
the merest solidity,
insufficient, what is called clay.

*

Out of all the whorls and eddies of air –
part of it sustenance
contributed by kale and dock leaves, anciently

the blue-green algae of bacterial seas, some of it
let out of the bag
to white out Montcalm or the western cwm –

comes the draught in Men's Medical this afternoon,
and all the fussing
with the window-pole, especially for the man across

who sits crinkled in foil, coddled in moon-boots
against his enemy,
which is yet also the old man's friend,

busy, and healthily scented here, always on hand
to be snipped
and walleted in the shallowing lung,

until nothing can be done with it,
                    until it pauses
at the lips, and passes, unexchanged

*

Out of the amorphousness of air, particulars,
                    nothing crystalline,
(and there are no 'instances') but

such as: *You are my heart's delight*
                    And where you ar – rre
I long to be – mac over the shoulder,

trilby pushed back – that was the style
                    but that was the man –
whistling along the street, hope springing

eternal, as you used to say, usually
                    satirically, defending
yourself against fortune too by exactitudes:

the slivers of tape on the radio dial,
                    the inks and keys
of clerking, the mortgage on the dot,

nothing done anyhow, till now –
                    . . .   . . .
O that you could catch your breath again

*

Nearly every night I meet you
in the underworld of dream.
You are waiting impatiently upon the lawn

or in the porch against the leaded glass.
'Yes, I have come at last.
Yes, you did all you could,' 'Yes, enough'.

Now, with every policy and scrap of adding-up in place,
from where you are,
you who felt the century so much closer to,

say, is there a future that you can foretell?
Some instruction?
Is there another library you can take me to?

You do not speak and cannot stay –
the porch is cold
even for stoics – here backs always turn eventually.

Which is why I keep your razor as it is,
your stubble still inside,
a tiny, capsuled drift – I cannot let it go.

It seems the last of you, but out of it
I change you back
and see you in a cloudless pool recovering length

by length that perfect crawl you never could quite teach
the shiverer, who is,
even so, left to himself, the better for your breath.

GHOSTS

The world – I mean the mind – is full of ghosts:
The husband, pronounced dead but palpable enough in bed
To hug, returns in bandages, his arm in a sling,
Beating at the back-door to be let in.

The world – I mean the universe – is full of itself:
Angles and relativities, compressions of the deep,
The steady tread of light bumping the earth, the waves
An abstraction of the nearly changeless sea.

Sometimes it can seem we are anywhere but here
Even though the ground insists upon it,
Stamps the soles of our feet to interrupt
How we would naturally be which is floating or falling.

ALL THE DEAD WANT

All the dead want of us is praise.

Or so we think.

Though words are crabby and coagulate,
embarrass us
                                        easier they are
than incontinence and phlegm.

We incise pure letters.
We walk to visit them.

We build them little towns, where,
when we have locked them in at night,
we fancy they might nod to one another,
sit on stools and knit
or furrow over football pools.

And we will speak well.
We will speak well.

But beforehand, blessèd are those by them in their desperation,
and that is bodily.
Blessèd are the hurried launderers
who lay on hands.

DOING PHILOSOPHY

Let the philosopher enjoy his dying –
It is his true profession after all: what he is
Readied for; it is the only knowledge and it's left till last.
Does it matter there is no speaking it?

Let the philosopher enjoy his dying
Despite the body's renitence at being
Put aside, its soaking of the sheets,
Its lamp-lace frailty, its brain in clouds.

For what could it do, this body, in its pomp?
Was there anything it could say it knew?
Any jealousy it could deny itself?
What was that beauty it stumbled on

But musk and appetite, like the bed on summer
Afternoons, even less complex than the purposes of flies
Haunting the will to fix them in their sorts?
Left to his mind he would not love you, dear.

So let the philosopher enjoy his dying –
Though there will be no thinking then
He knows we are a thought, not hapless bleeding.
It must not matter there is no speaking it.

THE SLOW BREATHERS

The slow breathers,
the saltie in Queensland
the tortoise on the lawn
live longer,

keep the gristly inside bark
of themselves
the less abraded,
the lacy sponge of the lung

in shape, admit errors more rarely –
the granulation under the eyelids
thus slowed down
for instance –

altogether roll more easily
with the regulation roughing-up
from oxygen, that happy, happy
synthesis of long, long ago.

BROKEN SYMMETRY

'... that the whole universe is never still for a moment...
everything is movement...'

Yes, everywhere, arcs in description –
San Lorenzo's tears of fire wiped once across the sky –
and beyond them the vermiculate heavens
whose nonetheless stolid beams
endure their march-time loneliness,
dispatch their resonances,
towards or away from us,
afoot with hares in the sallows, moles in the turf,
on one of the possible paths –
perhaps 'classical', perhaps not –
but in truth much as they seem,
else how would we watchers, who feel our time daily,
be here to spot the rates of change of rates of change?

*

As of the pool's aspiration always to stillness;
the blood's spiral stopping in your veins,
its cells no longer performing their virtuoso squeeze
through but settling for gravity,
the contusion gathering along the line of the bed;
though in your drying is still movement, moisture
only slowly given up to the desired default towards symmetry,
the pool's plane expanding its recovery from brokenness,
its grasp to have everything identified, singular,
to absorb the cut flowers in the vase
and the open Testament
into its peace.

Outside, the ranks of daffodils are racing.
Nightly he floats his clay-white face up to her.

TAKE ME BY THE HAND

Take me, someone, by the hand,
Lead me down the hill,
Put me by the fire's side.

The buses strain and skid on the cinders.
We totter and slip upwards.
My fingers, screwed tight,
Whiten from the tip.

Take me, someone, by the hand,
Lead me down the hill,
Put me by the fire's side.

ANNE'S SHELLS

i.m. Anne Alexander Davidson 1937–94

I say your shells though they are not really so.
I scooped them randomly from the beach
Plus a piece of blue crabber's twine as something
Of the place to tie you stubbornly in mind.

Placing them on a book page, I set to learning
Of their lives – identifying the teeth sockets
Studded on the hinge, the muscle scar of attachment
Where the body lay, its sinus sipping its goodness from the deeps.

This one will take so strong a tap it seems it is with us still:
Good morning brother scallop shell, kinned in calcium,
Self-assembled from the slosh we are,
Hard palate, hard ridge, bone of each other's bone,

Both so sturdy from siphoning our own patch of helpful universe,
The accumulate of a system whose glory is a finger nail,
The brick-by-brick, flight-by-flight of limes,
You particularised by the ocean's shrug, I likewise by the working air.

But we are not gold and time has already had some way with you.
At length what we will both together be is calx:
I, municipal tilth, you by incidentals
Abraded and raised elsewhere in the firmament,

And nothing can say this is just a different way to be,
That we can be content to be amalgamate again,
Spiting complexity, mindless in Poseidon's facelessness,
Gratefully lost in a shudder from Saturn's storms.

No, Anne, that is not where you are now,
Nor strolling in the gallery of forms, however configured
As Love, Justice, even Music, not gathered by rivers,
Not harmonical upon the prairies of the blest.

Nothing is better than to live – *inter homines esse* –
That is the synonym that stirs the ghosts to walk,
Makes the dead stretch out their thin arms to us
When we visit them – how could we beat them off?

They know what they are missing and that is it.
Living in the common sense of grief the fact is
You are not, no matter how much you visit by dreams,
Seem by surprise to be there at the table

And seem talkable to – you are not –
inter homines esse desinere – ceased to be among –
Desinent, to meet another word spiralling from
The gastropod into your absence

As, estuarine, byssus, sessile, evaporite.
Your shells lead me along a shoreline of information:
A few pages back, before there was Ynyslas,
Before there was Wales, out of the great swoosh

Of 'marine transgression', the taking and shaking of the earth
By chalky seas, then 'grave majestic Tethys' stepping back
As the Atlantic newly opens, building such details as
The Blue Point Oyster, *Crassotrea Virginica*,

And by the flick of a word stem I nudge you again
In what was called the Goodness of Virginia
Whose trees rained such rich and pleasant gums,
Which furnished such several kinds of flax,

The wapeih found so good for sores and wounds,
So many apothecary drugs, and vegetables 'far better
Than our English peas'. Out of all this came the health
And sprightliness by which you could turn cartwheels

In Edinburgh drawing-rooms – Summers at the shore,
The car loaded with the sunshines of America,
Passing Yorktown, Newport News – maybe the *Nautilus* out there
Test-diving in the roads – across the Chesapeake

And up 13, Cape Charles, Birdsnest, Jamesville,
Accomac, Modest Town, Temperanceville,
Chincoteague, the sand between your toes
On the beach where you are now sort of home again,

A modicum of outlandish, nearly-foreign calcite
Upon your National Seashore: 'Look for me
Beneath your feet' (your National Bard) – but does silicate, even
That anchoring beach-grass, truly show there is no death?

How many wake each morning, the wallpaper
Aged another night about them, and wish themselves
No more than the shell's abrasion,
At least no more than mechanical lingula,

The inarticulate, burrowed into the tidal flat,
Digesting the brack in as straightforward
A life as there has ever been,
Gentler by far than the sky waiting above the counterpane?

But this will not do. Though sand does get everywhere,
Into hair, socks, peanut-butter,
This is to be as fixed on the physical as when
In that summer in Galloway we could think of nothing

But midges, the children puffy, red and miserable,
All of us bitten to death,
And none of us philosopher enough to abide
The next itch wherever it was coming from.

Surely that seven-league stride – the mosses'
Maiden foothold, the worts breathing their first
To sweeten the gases into air, the millipedes'
Bronchial march – brought across the beach

Some spore that will eventually propose a mind
That can be comfortable with where it finds itself,
Undismayed that the body breaks,
Unimpressed by word of something liftable from its bones?

It would be so calm because so certain of the laws,
The power of lines and angles true everywhere,
Forever, which does not change and does not speak
And cannot be coloured in as the urgent angel –

Oh his golden head, his outstretched arm! –
Telling her how much better things would be.
At last will the universe have crackled,
But only to show how we are in motion and where

Exactly – 'There, there' – the indifference
Welcome because unwelcoming: we need not reply.
Summarised, sessile at last,
We could wait for that amen – could we?

But if that still is facelessness, and unbearable,
Watch Anne, and learn to bob on the unbroken deep.
Nothing about this will help us fathom it,
But learning to strike out upon it is our own storybook:

On pins, on tip-toe, until that moment –
The child races home to tell –
Both feet are off the bottom and holding on to
Nothing, frantic, grinning, paddling – but look, look!

To teach swimming is to be at work at life.
Here is the space I am, here is the time,
From where I will be in Lesson 1, standing on the side,
To breasting the swells running the creek towards me.

To teach a simple pleasure, a simple practice,
So someone can turn their back upon the deep
And float in the sun is an act of reason:
The space about me will be different, time will change.

In the pool or that miniature cove of the Pacific,
We see the world is not a hospital, nor an inn,
No kind of stop-over. To live is not to sit frozen
Before the fire or the blank of the fading wall.

Every stroke is an act, braving the trench
Below, and to show how to half-way master it
Brings joy to the tremulous child,
Goose-pimpled and improbable not an hour ago.

The gift is swimming, for the child one perfect point
Of alteration, a capability in the outside,
A splashy gait which is part of just themselves,
Some moments incommunicado, life-saving, learnt by exchange.

So, having lost another sock, on from Pwll Nofio they go,
Pellagra and the buboes long since conquered in their name,
To take their place in marriages
That mostly work, to stand behind counters,

To pick up the brochures yearly and do their sums,
Be hushed by news of sudden death,
Love their children, spoil their children,
Be damped into depression's anthracites,

Make a go of fitted kitchens, TV Repair, nursery teaching,
To be a fusilier as he always dreamed –
The first lost from his class, on the News it was –
Adopt a little Chinese girl who's doing fine,

Stop, unnerved, at the ward's overlapping doors,
Leave home, just change entirely,
Settle down at last – shorter than she'd hoped, and spotty –
Shoulder Oxfam's sacks and tallies in Libreville.

What are we doing, some of us, tonight, 8.7.97?
In the USA it is Janet's birthday
And the party must have started early
For John can't reach her on the phone.

He and we are eating an ordinary supper,
Save for the red wine, not usual for a Tuesday,
And – decent folk of Temperanceville as we are –
We make the jokes about that which have become traditional.

Ghana is not of course the place, if challenged,
I would now muster up in mind and it is there
Tom – after a day at work for water,
Up to his waist in a real *vita activa* – will be sleeping now.

Then John, the younger John, of whom his father says
'Who knows?' but no news means ok, will have left
His sleepless systems idling, but maybe finds himself
With a bucket under the eaves – freak storms in London apparently.

And at the neck of Chesapeake and Delaware,
Your father is still eager with the *New York Times*,
Your mother, white hair and her own mind still taut,
Gazes on the summer green as on that unseasonal snow.

And so on, across the ripple of all of 'us' –
Defined as who knew you – now cruelly going on,
Inhabiting these moments like the clatter of dishes does,
And the horn practice just starting now along the street.

STOIC

We are your friends, and, of course, willingly so,
Easily, because we love you for the quiddit
That is knowing you, all sorts of chewing-over:
What is surplus value? Could it be that additives

Are sedging the brains of kids these days? –
Look how they scream in checkout queues;
And cricket; and the running jokes of thirty years
I could not raise a laugh with here.

But when you've gone for the bus, and a minute later
I see it go by and wave, you look accidentally
Past me because already you are back
In what must be called your solitude.

Then, in a snatch of a waking dream,
Where the two of us are side by side in bed,
I see you outside, down the slope by the lakeshore,
The white of your cigarette in the dawn light.

This is, though you would not want to push the word,
Loneliness, which must be spoken to: *'I am at odds*
With how the world and its courses have dealt with me.
Somehow with its indifference I must be reconciled.'

RATIO

the clocks of coal
the clocks of lime
the clocks of sandstone, shale and schist

'What time is it?' she asked
                                        They filled the house
with Bach: *'Let us not divide…'*

                                        the welter of winds and
                                        waters
in their fractions
                    her slowed step
                              a few paces from the car

some pipework bustles in the wall

                              a winter fly stutters by the win-
                              dow-pane

a phone answered quickly

                                                  Where
is the denominator to recognise the consonance

of these intervals?

THE APPARENT COLONNADES

1

Across the red cliff, dotted in, stand the apparent colonnades.
The sun will know the truth of them,
How far they resemble basilicas or market-halls,
Whether an entrance might be concealed.
He will march through them fearlessly, knowing there is nothing
behind him, not even blackness,
For he never sees darkness,
Cannot conceive of shadow,
Has no need even to imagine a smudge.
He is where all such knowledge starts,
Semplice lume, somma luce,
All hues in all proportions,
Undivided and in no need of difference to see.

2

Compare the painter's muddle:
'The *apparent* colonnades';
The locomotive all at sea with steam and dusk, the firebox overdra-
matized upon the viaduct;
The fancy that at evening the walls and trees themselves dispense the
light;
That it was the artist's intuition that devised the still trapezist's
shadow on the wall.

Nor, given a subject, can any two of them agree just how it was:
Christ lies pinkly, greyly, austerely blind;
Christ poses spotlit among the shavings, like a five-year old at a party;
Christ folded into linen in so many different tombs;
Christ scrawny, ragg'd with spines, observing his armpit;
Christ in a dab of shadow, often a full poultice-paste of blackness, light
only allowed across his brow and the buffed shine of the black cuirass.
Somewhere, perhaps, a Christ sorry for himself, hiding under a table, a
little boy after all.

And, especially in executions, so much obscurity:
Who is this dark-furred judge presiding?
Who is this 'dead father', as wasted as by months entombed, roped to a
tree?
Does the curly-headed archer – foreground illuminated –
Think his shaded mark is Death itself?

3

But sunny Apollo falls upon all this evenly,
No sunkenness or hollowing,
Everything is there.
Thus he can pick out the unfinished hands of he who pulled a knife in a
robbery,
He who shot the man kneeling by the safe in *Kwik-Save*:
To that curve in the brain, the sickle shape of *vanitas* within the
male-factor's skull he penetrates,
And thus reassures the People's headsman,
Puts the felon to rasp brazilwood,
To the rope, the bull's pizzle, the hundred lashes,

To work the drowning cell –
Burning and grim he is, his eyes a domino of flame –
And so she should go down and dangle,
Peroxide bitch!

4

An argument should be approaching now
But only a cadence comes.
It rises to conclude that
We are all of us like painters and their kin,
All inside the light,
Only knowing what we know by darkness
And its feats of shadow.

It is a weak procedure for showing ourselves the world,
And still more for drawing out of our own heads such things as Justice –
That which we know we need but don't know the look of
Beyond that it is everything that is due,
And is strife, not vision (if we are tough enough),
And its every smudge is Tragedy,
All that is spilt, that could not become capable of solution, what makes
us gasp, terror –
Though we can turn that to advantage and wangle beauty from it,
The *chiaroscuro* Apollo has not a glimmer of,
A mood where we can ponder

Who is the cross-hatched old man sagging at the mark?
Does the dark-furred judge doubt he knows the facts?
Is the curly-headed archer praying 'Christ, Apollo, tell me this is right!'?

And what of the boy beneath the table
Who fears both the friends outside and friendlessness,
Fears both any kind of love and this solitude he seeks,
Who wants to be away, untouched in there, his own ragged splotch of life

Untamed by wisdom as she is practised?
He pulls the cloth down against the shiny afternoon,
Thinking he can keep it out, that he will not be seen,
And he is not.

He shoots the man he has kneeling by the safe in *Kwik-Save*.
This is where the argument and poem end.
How he would love simple, perfect light.

THE HUMANE HOUSE

'It is desirable that a man be clad so simply
that he can lay his hands on himself in the dark.'

At a knot-hole, looking inwards, ocean, land,
Beach and sky, everything outer, behind us,
If we watch faithfully we will see at length
Some wandering beam dawdle upon a shape within.

Thus Thoreau, walking one day along the Cape,
Beside the sea that comes ashore so
Indecorously, retreated from its inhuman tucks and turns
To seek and even enter that 'long-wished-for insight'.

So creased is his eye-socket against the grain,
He must believe that it is there: rolled round,
Concealed in the metaphor of a house for castaways,
Waiting on a patch of lamp-glass, the scratch on a tin plate.

Unless, as he watched, he felt a sand-grain cross his eyeball,
Sensed as he stood the contrition of all those
Unfleshed carcasses drive under the door and past the window-frame,
Filling the house, chasing apart the tinier and tinier

Crossways of light until they are holed up
And drowning between the close-fit slopes of sand,
Suffocated beneath a run-away now of beach and sky,
The last of light dragged first from our dwarfish sun

Then from the millions of suns still left,
Hoppered through the chimney, sucked through clapboard cracks
To be so crushed there will truly be nothing to see
And not even blackness to attend to.

What he had sought in an eventual gleam inside
Were 'the very bowels of mercy':
Some magnanimity, trust, practicality,
A gift of straw to make a fire out of the wind.

Instead he finds himself bystander at this last
Cataract of being. He unclasps his eye,
Wedges his feet in the sand and feels for his shirt-button
And a nubbin of flesh 'twixt thumb and forefinger.

FORM LAW ORDER SEQUENCE

Away from the tide's tucks and turns, educated Henry,
Looking out above his ghostly Shropshire sea
Wanted something that would speak from the shale
And suggest a sequence where he, who 'had just helped

Waste a million lives, more or less', could with his pen-strokes
Belong. He tapped and found the trilobites,
Impressive, thoughtful starfish 'whose kindly descendants'
He had back-flipped among in Quincy Bay,

An American in search of a father better than his father
And whom he could exceed towards perfection everlasting
Whether having come by lungs or gills no matter.
But it is only Change, he thought: at best the betterment

Of gooseberries, plumper, hairless, pinker at the heart;
Coal: power: the mortar hidden in peach-trees:
The sharp-shooter's last sleep. And he ceased to care
Whether the truth were true, putting it as flat as that.

ETERNI ANGELETTE AT WAVERLEY CEMETERY

Gaitano instructs,
but transliterating an unfamiliar hand
or mishearing the phonics,
the mason bequeathes disagreement,
'Eterni Angelette',
a stricken nicety,
to weather and all time:

Angelina giorni 7

and within twelve days

Mariuccia giorni 18

perhaps of some common fever
or tramway accident,
barely into the new century
the new country
this New South Wales.

So the pain cuts

nostre cuore
nostre figlie

who must never know the blight
of the chestnut trees
drying in the valleys,
or the white fields of Calabria

or wherever,

or the mattress dragging over the cartwheels,
never have that as *memorìa*,

but stand on tip-toe on this cliff-top,
in fresh space,
always eastward,
everything behind them
weightless
and surely in white.

And their Scotch or Irish boy,
or even Maronite,
will be clean and kind and work hard
in a tyre-bay or whatever,
build an extension,
make a good life,
and the girls would sit together here
pacìfico
pacìfico
watching their grandsons
catch the wave below.

This had Gaitano dreamed,
and kept dreaming,
lying beside them
each night,
hands still creased
with engine oil,
the ocean revolving down there
as he learned quarter by quarter
all the southern stars
until he died in English:

Father of the above
and beloved husband of Jessie Palise
who died 31 October 1936
aged 49

leaving incised
through weather and all time

Eterni Angelette
del nostro cuore
nostre figlie

'WAR POEMS': SIX PIECES

'The dead are unhappy enough as they are.
Is it necessary to dedicate laments to them forever?'

1 PRELUDE (FOR MOUTH ORGAN)

suck blow suck blow suck blow

when whippoorwills call

suck blow suck blow suck blow

and evening is nigh

suck blow suck blow suck blow

I'll meet you in my

suck blow suck blow suck blow

blow blue heav – en

2 NO HARP CAN WAKE THE WARRIOR

then heeled himself over the bolster taking
the print of his cheek and all the rest
lay down beside knowing there would be dreams
and that none would ever see again
their own folk or their borough streets
and walk out at night but hoped fortune
would find where they fell and see them carried
into the earth narrowed for their cot

and carried thus   into the earth
and that a porch would be raised   and a cup put by
that would gleam in the soil   as at the feast of life
when the burnisher lit   the night with his work
the reed sang   and there was plum and nectarine

May their trees   nod by that place
as long as there is time   between dark and dark

(after *Beowulf*)

3 PERSONAL EFFECTS (O SOLE MIO)

The Soldiers' Cemetery, Orvieto

Ti amo

Perhaps he does. And she him.
They've chalked it on the wall.
In ten years maybe they will be passing here to take
Their children to some treat or due solemnity
And smile sidelong as they pass.

For now, their condom, still heavy enough
Not to blow across the troopers' graves,
Lies here as some part of their story,
Maybe its closure . . . – *Ciao – Ciao* . . .
Beginning to perish across this lawn
Of splayed, parted or contorted boys
Who winked and grinned as well as died.

4 SOVIET POET READING (WORDS WITHOUT MUSIC)

This poet wears his laurels in his face.

Held together at the dressing-station,
under these lights it looks waxy,
mastic-yellow where it was built back
almost from the skull into the new man.

It will not move so much,
but the mouth will open
and would sing just for comrades,
the black dolls
of the KV cupola.

This poet wears his laurels in his face
but critically that cannot be –
his metres serve him, them, now us,
and he must not go
unsuspected.

We scrutators
of his lines and countenance
snigger or sneeze
sneeze or snigger.

5 THAT ROOM THAT SEA (ABIDE WITH ME)

I remember her white hair and her smiling
no one to be afraid of there   no uneasiness
through the dark afternoons alongside the snow-field
of her counterpane and pillows   save her bosom
and the steaming of the mighty poultices the blue nurse
prepared
pink ointment plastered across a rug of lint
the pain it must be   but she has to   'Go out now'

No one to be afraid of   but mauve drapes heavily held
she had been mad   I didn't know
locked up for a while
some buses turn off and go round that way
I was on one once   Who is this man
speaking to me suddenly with apron pan and spatula?

He was not from there   he is gone now
probably forever   the deep mauves and the window
on to what seems to be no outside
How could she smile so much?   when she had been
nothing
and he name rank and serial number   dysenteric
jam-packed in the prison-ship   the listing of her mind
her son roughly wrapped   brokenly spoken over
by whoever knew something of the words

6 SALVAGE (CODA...)

What happened
to the despised bristly khaki,
the battledress

of lancejack
humiliation and homesickness?
– Got rid of.

The old kit-bag
hung behind the door for years
for salvage:

paper and tins –
no ashes, egg-shells, no vegetable
matter.

On a waiting bus
one night – Cold Meece, the back-of-beyond,
by the R.O.F. gate –

the engine ticking down,
the reflections from the sparse bulbs
inscrutable,

out there in the
unseeable dark, already emplaced
in the soft fields,

the war came back,
coming in overhead, not with its flame
or clamour,

but its assumption,
its passage through walls, its filling
of the heart

so it can take
these souls, their nearest, dearest, their
hallway lights,

curtain pelmets,
non-drip gloss, chrysanthemums, new divans,
the D.I.Y.

of happiness,
of yearned-for, precious, modern life,
all

into oil-smoke,
polder, snow-drift, tideway,
notification.

That was a
future as it turned out; not this,
as it has

turned out, luckily,
and not exactly here, where my mind
can shake itself

as I remember
the bus start up and its lights
sweep the fields.

Nothing there,
some paper, plastic, brown glass,
green glass, clear glass.

from CLARITY OR DEATH!

I wish to God that I were more intelligent and everything would finally become clear to me – or else that I didn't live much longer!

LUDWIG WITTGENSTEIN

The progression of a painter's work, as it travels in time from point to point, will be towards clarity.

MARK ROTHKO

THE COFFEE STAIN

the coffee stain   I'll call it
      on your hip

the many washes of a spill
upon a tablecloth might produce
      just that shade and littoral

but haven't   so far as I am aware

expect by now a love poem
(whosoever might expect)

but what I am saying is not
to do with longing –
the ball of my finger across your nipple
and what would be the lightest touch there –

but with whatever is like and like
within *blotch* *dab* *patch*
and is necessary to think of
and beautiful and
like the loveliness of conjunctions
is nowhere

whereas on your hip is one shade and littoral

WE MAY BE ABLE TO REDUCE THE NUMBER OF DIFFERENT THINGS

I

Here on my little river-beach with Feynman
(he who professes the nose of a spaniel)
I practise the learned thought of how the local heron
will feel the same current in air as in water,
that this flow slips by the delta-wing,
rips the tide round Sark,
braces the fox as he sets
his mask for home,
and that all these can be understood together,
drawn in lines that themselves
bear nothing, move nothing,
yet, with just the faintest nudge for variables,
display the laws that bring the log ashore
like a heavy man.

II

It's foreign ground, the sand beneath the fox's foot,
river-borne to the beach by his sloping wood,
and he shakes it from him as he climbs back
into dry shadow and leaf-ground.
This outcrop under his paw could,
in some grindings, also be sand.
In a separate action,
rising with the moon,
the heron lifts
and folds itself back.
Moon, gritstone, sand.

III

Rule: there is no cagoule makes no noise.
But before that, much before our yap
and the dogs skidding in the leaves,
with, at most, the push of a breath
a hundred yards before
we have the heron's attention.

It's like a whisper into a dish
collected and conveyed,
like the bang on a can,
the scratch orchestra,
four minutes and whatever
of any sound,
and resolves with them
to a known line
which is in turn like the light wave,
a pond stirring, a hot wire,

the barchans of Turkestan,
the medanos of Peru,
and – we are bound to think this way –
fibrillation, quivering in the heart –
She used to say, *I can sit here*
and hear it pounding.

IV

Grace Crowley learned in Paris
(*ville d'art*)
to insist on the abstract elements

i.e. line, shape, and colour

i.e. (as I understand it)
what is 'inside' the 'given' space

'given' being a jug, a jar,
a tree, a mountain top

'inside' not cherries, *confiture* or leaf-vein,
and not the label, not the finger-post,
no matter how elegant the letter-form,
especially not the net weights in the glass

just volume:
how much is not
what is around it

and the lines
that mean this

soon less than lines

some shading

her ghost gum wore silver and the spinifex wore grey

v

to see enough in a few bottles vases and jars,
and to be so compelled says:
here must be the forms
beyond their instances –

and she is in a rage to paint
what she does not see –
from the wilds of the mind
air and light undefiled
so that the bottles vases jars,
though not inimical,
could be swept from the shelf
for they exist otherwise –

only
implying
other
bottles
vases
jars
even
every
one
possible

THE VISIBLE UNIVERSE CAN ONLY BE OF THE KIND THAT PERMITS US

Classically, this moment before the fox
ceases his assizing stare and disappears,
and the heron flaps diagonally to the opposite bank,
and I stop to try to arrest them, is *B*,
a 'point in time', the same in which
the moons of Jupiter, once thought unpunctual
but now recognised as early or late only according to
how near or far from us they are,
send us some particular light;
in which Sirius, borne in on itself
still signals outward; in which … (I could go on).
And *all* are arrived together from *A*,
that is point *A*, the starting point,
and must, by every bearing of the magi,
aligned with every known velocity
and thus made law,
have arrived here in just this order.
Although, *unclassically*, this has always been only
a possibility for there were many paths from *A*,
and few or none would have happened through
this *B* where the fox flickers into a darkness
that would be strange elsewhere,
full of air and built of shadow by just one sun,
held in all its places between sedate gravity
and wild escape,
and with all our fellow elementary dust still arriving
at *C*, which is again hospitable,
even if now cooling differently.

THE STARTING STATE OF THE UNIVERSE MUST HAVE BEEN VERY HIGHLY ORDERED

and even now, with fifteen billion years elusive cooling –
this slow frustration of the boilermaker's art –
the vixen does not find herself with eggs,
the heron need not peck blood to feed her cubs,
once more the comet meets its ETA
and camper-vans assemble for the great eclipse.

Yes, there is *the stealth, the violence, cunning of the sea*,
as there is junkyard DNA, and Poe's odd conchology,
but we that know we nothing were so long,
– *beneath the dust did in a chaos lie* –
and are of a mind to feel the quantum shudder
need not be afeard: the particles do body-pop
and jostle in our sight, but still heed
their codes and nice formations,
and will reorganise tomorrow as we die.

THE UNIVERSE IS LIKE A POOL THAT HAS HAD A STONE THROWN INTO IT

And like a high black tarn resuming itself
the ripples would pass away,
land and sky swim together,
that man who by the red dot of his jerkin
can just be seen heaving a heavy cask aboard
will be washed into the land, the land
into the brown sea, into the sky

which might till lately have been likened
to sacking purged of every shade and stain,
every snagged thread and lump-knot,
but now removes itself and every likening,
even the ideas of stitch and knot,
dissolved with the stars into

default   the restitution of all
things
                                        when we speak of peace

'Then is the seriousness of life done away with,' said B.

'I am going to rejoin the Real,' said A.

ALL THE ORDERED FORMS OF ENERGY IN THE UNIVERSE WOULD ULTIMATELY FIND THEMSELVES DEGRADED

The effort of the heronry and earth
arrests disorder, at least that of the random twig
snapped out of its purposeful economy:
thus is its messed-up, evaporating energy
re-applied and the tidy nest
postpones   the inchoate –
      heaven and earth passed away
imagined as buzz   drone   background

But that is coming, though it will not come,
for there can be no point of arrival
even though the cost borne by the nest

in the burn of starch and sugar
is given off without recapture.
It seems a heel-and-toe business,
and they raise their young. But at length
the housekeeping goes awry, the heronry
is deserted, the ground unlit, untenable,
and always the measurable tendency is outward –
a feather lost and blowing away,
every star passing to the same consistency –
a *purity* it might be called in some quarters.

OH! OH!

Oh! (and Oh!) this pretending to the void!
this always being sweet
on the pebble-dashed nebulae,
this peddling of (and into) the sumptuous blue,
the razor-slash – *uh! uh!* – struck through
into blackness,
beyond, beyond,
always the space beyond
as though there is a nothing we can know
that will not cool, carbonise
at least into a dot, a splotch, a word,
not always some thing,
be it so indefinite, so infinite
as balance upon a beam, or on a wire across the
– *ahem* – where the artiste takes his tea

everywhere else is not mystery it is death

THERE MAY BE SYMMETRICAL UNIVERSES BUT THEY ARE NOT OURS

You always knew sir, didn't you,
that what we see and draw cannot exist?
However wide our local heavens can become,
no conjunction and no crystal, however deep,
will give us a circle unbubbled at its edge,
a triangle in precise equipoise,
an any-hedron that is not anyhow,
even fleetingly, because
though *symmetries break reluctantly,*
they break, ours break certainly,
and thus the measuring begins,
even if we were barely shuddering here,
and we are not.
But please still see them sir.

A POINT IS NEVER ALONE

I

In Mr Cooksey's Technical Drawing class dots would never do.
Joining up two soft-pencil puddles of lead
will get you from where to where?
And if your line is a stubby 5B thick,
a dimension *we* can see never mind dust-mites with their wagon-trains,
where has it arrived?

Draw like that and your tea-tray will be wonky,
your screw-thread strip itself,
your piston grate in your cylinder. *Snigger snigger.*

So, first, the perfection, over weeks in the Woodwork Shop,
of the sandpaper block.
Now a good 4H could be shaded fine enough
to make a hairline cross,
and the narrowest line could join them,
just as in geometry, where your pencil should also be sharp –
Sharp, boy, sharp as the point of your compasses –
and places that have no parts or magnitude –
that do not exist –
will arrive at your desk here on the top corridor
as squares, triangles, parallelograms,
and, between these non-existent points,
we get a table-lamp we can take home.

II

but there are still hikers afoot
across the finest line:
on and on, (or down and down)
the point descends,
a sea-stack of the hardest lead,
within it the same magnitudes
as of the universe to Earth,
Earth to atom, nucleus to whatever,
are vibrating there and on to wherever gravity
is seeping to, to whatever is happening to time

– When are we stopping sir?
Please sir, Mr Cooksey, we cannot believe in nothing.

III

musicians wrestle everywhere
as do the numberers, their kith and kin,
who starting, perforce, from here,
would rise and bring the nearby wanderers
every shovelful of dust,
every passing flare of hydrogen
into a reckoning
so they can rock together,
swing to the same algorithm:
the falling almond
and the furthest curvature.

And it will be true:
the Form of things,
and most beautiful because
it is its indifferent self,
recognised only in our imaginings

knows nothing

but in our staunch imaginings

IV

Why did I choose almonds as an image
in this advocacy?
Certainly because I have this tree to sit beneath,
its scatterings are many though not a myriad –
they will not do, for instance, for stars.
Custom of poem and the summer's chance
bring the almonds into work.

You could say thus was it written,
but also that the almonds that are not stars
fall randomly on to this page as on the grass.
The thought of almonds and the thought of stars,
or the thought of samphire cut and out for sale,
the collarless recluse with his cellar junk and firewood,
the man with the ear-scar in the Services –
Star and almond and their various velocities,
yes, well, their tandem will be seen,
but then the samphire, and the men,
which could be waves alone and never caught upon the gel?
Collar, cellar – ok ok
that's a function – let's now extrapolate
the shifty universe of albumen and stars.

BY CATEGORIES DO WE MAISTER [MASTER] THE WORLD

we always think that we are looking on looking in

that it is in us to see

that it is the long-nosed mouse underground
gobbling the artichoke roots
that the diamondback's a heat-seeker
that we can read the broken sand
revealed by dawn
the scutter-marks and fine-drilling
all for food and danger

we always think we are looking on looking in

sand   scutter   snake   snout-mouse
if we speak them they will be –
and made ours by arrangement

the bones rattled cunningly in a cup
scutter across the baize till time runs out
and 'warming' will work for any creature
of the genus ectotherm (though it must be tested)

and skink shall beget skink unto the last generation

yet we are made lonely by our categories
for nothing else owns them

FACTS: I BOUNCE MY BALL

I bounce my ball against my stone
I bounce my ball against my stone

for you this wall is real, a fact,
and 'brute' in that for all your powers
you cannot pass through it,
and that its stones, like its cousins in the gorge below,
need no requirement of yours to be

the water there also is 'brute': it cut the gorge
and could drown you, even though
the dam now holds it in the concept 'lake',

though I would not call that 'institutional' exactly,
not like a coin from the excavation
which will fall helplessly through every slot
but still belongs to 'money', and you know
how real that is, the part it has in digging the clay,
logging the forest, firing the kiln,
trading the ware downstream,
the dishes, the bowls, the amphorae
for oil *for* wine *for* dinner
and how all conurbations need
customs and laws which will also be brutal
but only exist because you say so
for even when engraved a law is not a stone

I bounce my ball against my stone
I bounce my ball against my stone
I bounce my ball against my stone

WE SO LOVE THE LAWS

we will rush into crazy houses
into the pill that makes us small
shriek at mirrors that draw us out like gum
or smear us across the glass
knowing it's all four-square really
your Harlech Castle your Tower of London
load-bearing up to the attic the skylight the stars
some of which we know will be where we find them

or they might, like this world does, say:
You know I am here, but then shuffle
so 3 will not follow 2
the lift might go in any direction
the turn-right to the shops
will not be the same turn-up tomorrow

so I settle on tapping the same tooth for hours
look at one horseman in the carpet forever
I hear this noise *uv uv uv uv* but there's nothing in it
what is this at my skin?

AGAINST THOSE WHO REFUSE DEFINITIONS

Let us set foot aboard the trireme and I will say
it is a man, you will say it is a wall
while the captain holds fast to his oar.
Or – no. So, to refer to recent cases, let us simplify
and say a heron and a river are the same thing
and that therefore you can step into the same fox twice,
whether it be that one this morning fleeing from the bins,
this one in the knitting pattern or even that Basil Brush,
although he pretends to a name all his own.
Thus undefined let's say they and we
are all things together, just as the old heron
when at last it stumbles and drowns
is obviously the river, just as we are so much water,
just as the trireme will have its wooden walls
as Nelson did 'gainst Reynard and his crafty crew.
The captain tries to hold fast but we yaw.

Next week we will come on to galley-slaves.

WHAT NEED WE KNOW OF THE WORKINGS OF NATURE IN ORDER TO APPRECIATE HOW CONSCIOUSNESS MAY BE A PART OF IT?

there will most likely be a rule

but

I do not think an earthquake thinks
as I think,
nor the coral, nor the wasp's nest

for instance I think I can decide
whether to dive today: yes or no
it feels simple enough
and started only this morning –
it does not feel as though a billion steps
have come to this:
I will / I will not
flop off the stern today

then suppose otherwise: suppose I've burnt my foot
and this black tissuey skin is shredding
by rule – not one that 'decreed'
I would burn my foot today,
but one that said
the cells will fall this way
and this way shares a property
with the growth of coral and the wasp's nest
and even with the shuffling of plates
or dominoes?

FAITH IN REASON IS THE TRUST THAT THE ULTIMATE NATURES OF THINGS LIE TOGETHER IN A HARMONY WHICH EXCLUDES MERE ARBITRARINESS

the periodic tiling of the wasp's nest, or coral

but then a fox under the breakfast table

and faith in the order of things
takes a knock,
                                        though it was,
as you would expect, running for its life
at the time so there will be a thus and thus

does this mean that as I descend the page
the arbitrary must always elude me,
that however much I strive to be undeliberate,
cut paste and randomise or go automatic
out of dreams or dominoes,
or the thoughtless ingenuity embodied
in the mouse, the arrival of Kirkland's
Warbler here, or August as Kintore,
though yet to be understood by you
could be, should you be interested enough?

What would really count?
Can I who's seen my Dad take the coal-hammer
to treacle-toffee and a Christmas nut
act words no explanatory power on earth could crack?

Stop it now. We cannot have faith
in the arbitrary, though some profess it,
and are happy that freedom must equal chance.
Are they more comforted than those of us
who long for it all to *lie together*?

THE ABSTRACTION OF NUMBER IS BEAUTIFUL

Take *five*: drums, bass, rhythm, lead and vocals
in a pub in Ashton-under-Lyne,
or Newcastle-under-Lyme,
Hell's Kitchen, a garage in Texas,
a dark park in Dortmund;
Matthews McIlroy Mortensen Mudie Mitchell,
though they can never have played together –
would that they had (only for Stoke though);
Napoleon's victories: Austerlitz, Eylau, Jena,
Wagram, Borodino – *Borodino? Not so fast*,
says Tolstoy: ... *cloudlets of smoke ...*
historical science in its endeavour
to draw nearer to truth ... the smell
of saltpetre and blood ...
Gimme five, 'I'll give it foive', top five, first five,
five-star, Five-live, fish alive, more than, less than,
(trochaic five), best of five, starting five: Frazier, Bradley,
Barnett, DeBusschere and Reed – (iambic five? not quite)
but they did play together, and didn't they play Terry?
and I see you in a dream on 5th above Fifth

your jump shot fading to the basket …
five for the symbols at your door,
brag, stud, par, petals, loaves, parts of the body.

Here – independent of all *things* –
is the use, wonder and beauty of what we cannot see

…AND WITH THE INDIAN FIGURES 987654321 AND ZEPHIRA ALL CALCULATIONS ARE DEMOCRATICALLY POSSIBLE

I

We could *by algorisme tell the gravell of the sea*,
though would such a use count among its treasures?
Written in the sand, the tens and units would stretch along
the shore,
but its few strokes still economise on abacists.
Without *zefira* there was nothing,
no way of writing nothing;
with it every distance,
every credit, every debt,
and how the universe bends round itself:
the decrees of physics are the decrees of fate.

II

That so much and so many could be hidden
in these ciphers, that is the mystery the Saracens
have brought us in *sifr*, *zefira*,
a breath of the west wind,
yet less even than that;
the bundled sticks of stars, the gravel sets:
zero, *shûnya*, empty hands, nothing

III A REAL SUM IS A SUM OF REAL PEOPLE

But I can catch a chill, an *algory* indeed,
as I glimpse something fearful in ciphering,
what those might have meant who called it
easy Satanism: the million dead
so easily summ'd up:
neither one nor two nor three
but a poor cipher.
We can be who we are
but *other men stande for no more than Cypheres*
in Algorisme – they are the versatile sand-wave
and do not stand.

THE WALL THAT SEPARATES THE LIVING FROM ONE ANOTHER IS NO LESS OPAQUE THAN THE WALL THAT SEPARATES THE LIVING FROM THE DEAD

After a couple we wave and say goodnight to S,
half-under the porch, one shoulder
of his Oxfam zoot-suit
black with rain, his too-small baseball cap
pushed up on hair you'd think
was treated daily with cement-dust,
the can in his hand,
and he says *G'night*, as though
we could see who is standing there,
as though he could walk through the door
of The Oak without needing to be
bold as brass, as though there are no
walls of brass between him and the barmaid
and the horseshoe of drinkers debating
how you run cars on cooking-oil.

Does he more easily walk through walls
with a pack-mule,
and cross the lobby unmolested,
and find his Gran, or whoever it is
he may want to see, up in her room
with everything tidy and smoothing out
her best dress to welcome him?

MERE BAGATELLE

... sometimes, out of the corner of an eye, 'at the moment which is not action or inaction', one can glimpse the true scientific vision: austere, tragic, alienated and supremely beautiful. A world that isn't for anything, a world that is just there.

Jerry Fodor

1

the usual thing would be
to look up at night –
there, there, there it is!
or, more often now,
to squirrel into the lawn –
there, there, there it is!
somewhere under the nail

must it still have names?

no, leave that aside –
there is this idea
of its beauty

2

the stars are nearly perfect
(for this)
they have a sort of light –
bare-faced metallic,
as seen in dark, grey-brown sand –
and their famous twinkling

is like a blind smile
that is ideal
for their ignorance

even if they are caught up
in what admits,
in what permits us

3

but that we are permitted
does not mean
that anything is counted,
still less provided for

this fact can be called 'austere'
as in 'an austere regime'
or 'that was an austere look
she gave me'

4

so what could be the
paragons by which
to see ourselves?

the gods nagged
and are gone –
discontinued the huffers-puffers,
randy, watery, windy, owl-eyed,
blood-drenched interferers,
presidents of rocks, springs,
boggart and quarry-holes

(see how easy this
embellishing is?)

though even with just the One,
who has no body,
parts, or passions,
a tossed date-stone
puts out an eye
and starts some tale running

5

(*though*, like *so nevertheless thus*
therefore sometimes however but –
is going, loosely speaking,
to be a problem here throughout;
along with *one can*,
and especially *we*
as in *we* do [smell the mint]
– *who* does? me and Lindsay Lohan? –
we think [if lintily];
but I do *know* –
we do know this don't we? –
that I AM WRITING A POEM
[some of us like to be reminded
of this at regular intervals:
it makes us feel justified somehow
it seems; but more do not
and think conjunctions
adverbs prepositions
are such presumptuous
abstracted devils –
they want to smell the mint!]

but, even here, in poem,
we are not saved
from cogitating –
and anyway if you think on things,
Lucretius said,
it'll learn you to relax,
and Virgil,
he found verses appropriate
to advise on sheep-dip)

6

there is a shoot of stones
or swallows,
the fringe-drops
of a storm

there is number
or there is not

7

than that there is,
nothing is more surprising
in Nature

than that we find it anyway
nothing is more surprising
in Nature

(this has been noted more than once)

but, either way,
are they, the figures,
austere enough?

8

when Mr Preece taught me to count,
each numeral stood on the clock
as golden and as palpable
as he in his railways wais'cot
with its 6 crested buttons,
or as the troughs
in next door's greenhouse
the handfuls of hard tomatoes
the weights and scales
the raised iron blisters
of av'rdupoise

no, never austere enough

9

since no two tomatoes
on the scale,
no two globes we know
are the same,
is it they,
or the idea of the sphere
that is beautiful
if we do just catch sight

of our Creation?

10

see also John Ruskin's drawing-lessons:

'set yourself steadily to conquer that round stone,
and you have won the battle. Look your stone
antagonist boldly in the face.'

11

most of what is beautiful
cannot be so –
we say swallows
diving and cutting
are beautiful
then recognise
their labour
in an early dusk;
the silk-worm's spinning,
the bat-hawk's streaming upwards
are hard yakka,
desperate even

and all our stories
are desperate:
narrow escapes
and passing saints,
how to recuperate
the unhappiness of girls,
or taste their sorrow

perhaps it must be
what is most
inanimate:
it is Rafaello's line,
twenty centimetres
over the brow
to the throat
that makes
his madonna care
but without what we hope for
of maternal love –
take away the child,
what happens
to the line?
is it then
a scratch on a wall
where a truck reversed?
human art

always winks at us

like this,
teases like
an irregular tapping
quite distant
and out of sight

so what, among
the mathematics
where we live, is
unaffected,

as far from ladies' slippers
as can be?
certainly
it must stand
without us:
in balance
and with nothing
remaindered

but why do we wish that?
why, when we like the line
that seems beyond us,
but is not?

12

there are things we used to call blessèd
meaning damned:
bootlaces, wallpapering,
knitting, plug-wires,
anything that can get
into a robble

blessèd is the way we are here
as the world surrenders
such of its simplicities as gravity
and the jigger for red hair
etcetera etcetera
but goes on and comes back for more

13

such words are still with us,
mostly for talking to those
who cannot hear or cannot reply
or who are truly busy

blessèd now are the micro-explainers
the improvers of sutures

the peacemakers obviously
where they can be found

of course it's not stupid
to talk to no effect

14

meanwhile
on they go,
the *vast Rondures*,
swimming past Neptune,

and the base pairs
and the conserved sequences
and our surprising cousin yeast,
copying itself, varying, selecting
and thus going on,
and I will call him cousin
not just to humble us,
but because he must be found a place
in the saga

15

but again,
what would the saga be
in which we do
meet ourselves?

it should be a story
of good heart:
of cousinhood or uncleship –
let me listen, let me
for a brief while
lay down
this solitary bachelorship
of mine

that should be the lyrics
book and score

16

if it is not,
if that cannot be assured to us…

who could bear a story
where her imprisonment
was never at an end
where both were eaten
by every dragon
where we are the giant's
footfall
and feel nothing
but his rage?

each of these would be
a story that returns us nothing,
as where the souls
are harried and fly
but never move

17

after Leonid Lerman, 'The Last Man' (i)

this clay that stands in
for the human head
is true

though it does not cry
it is tugged up
to the side

and it is lettered:
basic Latin, Arabic–
extended, Hebrew,
Cyrillic, Greek –
pressed, incised,
ledged into
scabbed on to the clay
by now with every bit taken

it must want
to be read

18

after Leonid Lerman, 'The Last Man' (ii)

perhaps he is stamped
with broken names,
one among them his own,
and this is his torment –
how many names
can a man bear?
each lost,
mislaid,

vous avez perdu l'homme
il faudra le retrouver
ce ne sera pas facile

you (?) have lost man,
he must be found again,
it will not be easy to do

19

time then for the man
at least as perfect
as the stars,
or at least as sheer,
'bare-faced metallic',
and with a modern purity

he will be unwritten

he will carry nothing
on or about him

as he progresses,
as he lifts each foot,
the step will be erased

he will need nothing
to care for

he can live here

he will just be here

20

taking the sun apart
has proved the easier
the advice was clear
and has been heeded:
wait and watch,
let the universe
with all its
unnamed stars
and coloured sands and soils
think us out
and then bow
as the cards are time-lapsed
across the palm
elegantly,
and certainly

– tired anyway
of the great logics
embowelled
in us

21

though what is in us
was once without us,
'out there' until
whipped up from dust
till we are like we are now,
djinns careering,
small clouds
forming and reforming,
adjusting stars,
erecting our systems
of stones and flowers
high and low,
racing to the ship pursued,
struggling
with our law-making
like bathers
with their clothes,
and with all the styles
of love:
vast exaltation,
and the children our gift
locked in the car
and asphyxiated
along with him or her

22

after Alberto Burri

if I see the universe
as a piece
of sacking
half a metre square
used and re-used
snagged
knotted
jabbed with red paint
an oil-drip
some stencilling
and that's all,
I am in error

in the way that I am
unnatural though,
that is what I see

23

words, and other
of our imaginings –
lines, sounds –
are the confounding
of Nature –

enough already,
cries She,
of Jairus' daughter (12)
and the combing out

of hell,
or even Homer
Simpson squeezed
through a worm-hole
and escaped to tell

these are uneven and
unfinished doings,
grass cuttings,
mere bagatelle

24

how little creates
it seems:
a dot, a fast line,
and with the right smudge
the painter can get
a window certainly,
a distant deckchair,
another and another one,
and then the naked board
can serve untouched
as a beach for the people
who are there too,
one hopping
into trousers,
another dozing
with a book

the pier-lights
are coming on,
greasepaint
cane and fedora
a soft-shoe
a sad face,
and it's all purple now,
the audience
laughs as one,
like a dog's abrupt
once-over shake

25

so if we see this
true scientific vision,
is all then calm?
can we chill
like Lucretius said?

well, death still *devours*
and is called noisy,
the rapids' savage chatter,
and we, all of us,
waiting and wailing

but to know
that the moon
is not in fact
in travail,
that the winter sun
is not day by day
the more distracted

and incapable,
but to see that yes,
it's short-winded
but not so far advanced,
and remission is likely,
does this lighten our step
and refresh us?

if we can see through –
then blessèd are we
– and I mean lucky now

26

for all that happens is this:
microscopic variations,
macroscopic effects:
the classification
of regularities
is what it's down to

thus the airborne bacofoil
(as it would become)
for Cockburn's
phantom fleet
departing Dover;
thus Bernal with all
that could be known
of wave-motion
off Colleville-sur-Mer,
already in his pocket
grinds ashore
and is gathering samples

re tank-tracks
by D-Day + 1
(or so he claimed,
Solly, later Lord Zuckerman,
pooh-poohed it –
so was he there
or wasn't he?);
thus the penicillin moulds
for the dressing-stations;
thus the burn-rates
of wallpaper;
thus the war won,
thus Science and Society,
it all adds up,
sand tide and air,
rates and percentages
everything connects,
and here's Professor Leakey on
God's inordinate fondness
for beetles,
their giant success,
and the dangers
for shirt-fronts
of eating mangoes,
hence the logical
advice to eat them
in the bath

27

after Riccardo Reis

to be so imperturbable
would be to be
something soughing –
alliteration again,
it stole up on me
again

but I am not
to be laughed at,
this is my little rage
for order,
balance,
I do not want
to fall off

a poem should be
a paean
to law and order –
what else is there?
justice?
a 'land of'?

'soughing' is always
as of the wind,
was when *swōgan*,
do not be perturbed,
there is always the wind,
button up your overcoat

28

to see the soul of Nature
in the forms of matter –

sounds heroic,
but is it best,
knowing how things are,
to be always about the house
interpreting?

the mechanism
does not need us for this,
there is nothing latent
requiring us,
we are free for now –

there, there, there
it is!

29

what means anything
is dispersed:

a badge or bones
stirred by a plough

the woods still seared
from when a man
drove in, parked
and set himself alight

30

what is not austere,
and what is not true,
and what is not stupid
to say,
is folded in your note,
to be found in the event,
in your special box,
which – paraphrased – says:
when you read this
I shall have gone
to be with your father again,
that is where I really
want to be

this is the kind of way
we look at death,
it is not – especially when
elaborated – austere,
and it is not true,
and it is not a stupid thing
to say

31

the figure raising his arm
in the main boat
is possibly a self-portrait

but why would he
be doing with that
when it is the deep
and the sky
that matters here?

raising his arm
can barely be seen –
is he awaiting
a detail of the painting?
even then how much description
would he need
to be himself?
more than a belt, a hat
and a shirt – in fact
there can never be enough
which is why I don't believe it –
look, catch sight of me! no

sadly, perhaps,
he has given up his ghost
to the deep and the sky
and to what light does to him,
if not yet renounced
what the composition
requires,
which could be
a raised arm

32

real, not mum
's the word that taunts us
since there's no end to it
and no end of it
for the world –
to say no more –
is very full
and no one can tie it,
like a cord of hickory or stone,
and carry it home,
or even, if they are honest,
say this or that will do
to stand in for it
tempting as it is
to start figuring
with this cicada,
at sea on a clean shirt,
as I use a straw
to lead him
at least as far as
the washing-line
(the kinder philosophers
are said to set down
their caterpillars)

O blessèd thing,
save yourself!
O world!

still trying
to catch a glimpse

33

real though will do better
than most words
to humiliate –
all those worlds
I, you, he, she
do not live in:
the coalmines
of cake and milk,
the steel bowls of truth
at which we scrub and scrub
and never see ourselves

34

the stone will not
remember for us,
we have to perform the office:

enter the miserable
grammatical dream
where Cain says:
there is no judgement
and no judge and no other world;
therefore there is no good reward
to be given to the righteous,
and no punishment
for the wicked,
and in the hollowing of the stone
drives a stone
into his brother's brow
and slays him again

and again

knowing that everything is
just fretwork
should free us
from all that,
except we should not be
freed

35

our word for today
is *system*

Dad liked systems
of his own devising
such as those
for the filing of guarantees,
the storage of plant-pots and raffia,
booking the south coast
Allocation Train,
the Allo-cation Train

all this seeks and defends:
go on spec and you could be
out on the street
at 7 in the morning
and what we want
is all the three of us together
with a song in our heart
along the prom prom prom
tiddly-om-pom-pom
and everything going
according to plan

36

could he have thought
of himself as *system*
in the sense of whole,
everything for the use of
added up
divided with no remainder
a place for everything
like ashes and compost
and salvage?

no, he could not,
could not keep his hair on,
and who can?
he knew that what ought to be
is not, and though
systems of shoeboxes
and pastille tins
did help the three of us
live together –
do not disrespect
such things' place
in harmony –
they are defiance only,
and longing:
let the world
be settled up like this

some hopes
was a favourite phrase he had,
some hopes I still like to have

37

sometimes … one can glimpse –
like the rising
or setting sun
will catch a window
twenty miles away,
toy with it,
have it dance and blaze
in rapture
or immolation
until the angle shifts
and again it is
workaday glass?

we know how we saw this,
and how it happens,
but what it was
in the sense of
substance,
something you could cup
your hand around
like other flashing lights
on tractors or road-works,
is something else again

'Goggles', the painter,
'Speccy-four-eyes',
painting himself to look out
of the mirror
as though it is a witness-box,
alleges that that's the way it is:
the world does not front up,
plant itself

like a bouncer in a suit,
and give us time
for our assizes

look! something else like it
again, a little sashay
on the kitchen floor

and gone

like a cat over a wall
like a lizard past a stone

38 EPILOGUE

For [my emphasis] *thee*
the world of fragrant flowers is drest,
For thee
the Ocean smiles and smoothes his wavy breast
and Heav'n itself
with more serene and purer light is blest

and, as well:

How EXQUISITELY the individual Mind
(And the Progressive Powers no less of the whole SPECIES)
To the external world is FITTED.
AND how EXQUISITELY too
the external world
Is FITTED to the Mind.

– Did you hear?
– What?
– That
– What?
– *The sunbeam said, 'Be happy.'*
– Really?
– *It loves us now, this Vale, so beautiful, Begins to love us!*

Now read on:

39

there is an abyss of words
approaching
but no notice:

how can an abyss
approach?
I do not know,
I am not responsible
for the exact phrasing
only the re-use
but the ground
is softening
becoming spongy
elastic, springy

O world!

now read on

CALL DEATH AN OBSERVATION

I

call death an observation,
a supplied fact, ever more precisely noted,
(though mistakes have been made, ask any Goth)
and some vital sign may still be missed –
a monitoring may be merely mechanical,
conducted dozily after lunch, or not adhere
to best practice –
but from the many instances
the law 'We Die' has been induced,
and if shaggy at first, improvised –
and may still be so compared with
what might be to come – is now deduced,
the maths showing us how much we can infer
of what we do not know

it seems irrefragable, and as long as the law
coincides with observation it holds

II

if lines and circles are all our own work
have we invented death?
motionlessness seems to be
what was decided upon,
that she or he could no longer shift for herself
and would just dry there
or deliquesce depending,
although many (most?)

have traditionally not gone on such appearances
but when forced to give up say:
but this is not the real line,
what is real has no lines
because no space or time
because a line must be an act in time
and mind

because it is not bearable
to live with lines and circles

III

mathematics makes up the bolus,
what could be truer than such proceedings?
the equations of fluids in and fluids out,
the charting and cross-checking
towards a line to be pronounced upon:
the baby-like milky regurge
at the corner of the mouth,
sent out, uncalibrated, bubbling slightly

but somewhere there the point –

it happens always and the line is true

*

and before the May-dawn, the conventional dream-ship,
bulk cargo freighter, or sharp-prowed liner,
the black *Normandie* or another such,
seemingly unworked, eyeless, unhurried;
and knowing you cannot row aside

from *THE REASONER*

1

History could make a stone weep

John, what takes you back to Evensong so late?
Did History fail you?

I, who have spent no time at all in archives or the field,
have to say it is still the Book of Where Things Happen,
The Book Endlessly Corrected, the Book of Witness,
The Book of Expectant Understanding.
It absorbs us and it should.

*

When Deian's mobile went off
I heard you guffaw from the coffin.
That's a fact. No it's not. Who else heard it?
But how much impartiality should we try for?
I'm talking *to* you John, not 'for' you…

… sometimes in 'conversational French':
… *le grand vin blanc de Bourgogne… la grammaire*
des civilisations… how *actuel* is
le monde actuel?… does it just roll through us,
and by the by absolve us from any blame attached?
How much impartiality should we try for?

*

Surprising you in the backmost pew,
I'm curious to know if it be the music or the words?
Can I catch you murmuring *Now lettest Thou…* ?

Thou of whom it is said: *Thou* knowest all things,
Of whom it is said: *Thou* canst do all things
Of whom it is said: is in all things just
Who will grant us grace

because we find we are not
and cannot do these things

as History shows

and need these things

as History shows

at least to imagine them

as History shows.

And we are not absolved.

*

John, reason with me,
am I hearing you aright?

2

Starting early with my dog, boundlessly,

or on a solitary walk by a riverside,

or in a stew or a studio, or in a stew in a studio
a proper brown one,

you will find me.

But am I the same in your eyes as in mine,
or in that third eye, the barber's captious glass?

My dome is as innocent, as artless, as a wig-stand;
the elastic that fastens my spectacles has crimped one ear;
I am spry still but stooped from the books I bear,
a few good bindings but glue-split paperbacks mostly,
bundled, strapped and wedged into packs, fardels,
so that philosophers laugh as I waddle by.
Also about me: pyramids, cubes and squares,
a wood-gauge and a rule, as Don Quixote says:
'in my profession
you must know everything'.

I am one who would know,
and thus be happy.

3

A single filament of a spider's web
only appears because of how
for these ten minutes the light plays it,
like the back and forth of a slide guitar
as it is caught in the vagaries
of the tiny wind.

Nothing else anywhere, ever, has these,
offers these same movements to an eye.
Hard to grasp how this thread and light as seen
is 'intellectually inferred'.

But looking at one thing am I missing another?

4

Beliefs are necessary, I do believe.
There is enough white water and storm scum
to show that life is not a book group
or a week in a hammock.
Not that abeyance is a crime:
it may be praiseworthy, principled even,
enabling us to hang out with whatever
and whoever we please for the while;
in some desperate circs. it might even keep us alive.
But… but… 'but' will butter no parsnips
in the end, and should doubt doubt doubt,
as it surely will, there is only 'and so on

and so on and so on' until, as sages keep saying,
'all I know is that I know nothing' –
I really do believe that – *oh my, do I?*
Oh yes indeed I do.

5

5–9 in memory of René Gallet

Is our language complete? Not on your life!
Not like H2SO4. Not like the law of sines
with its allowance for the ambiguous case.
But there is the hope

the *one who hopes*

for simple agreements,
perfect understanding
for nothing not ever irregular

In Stoke-on-Trent post-war we were keen on Esperanto.
Here, where breathing could be difficult,
was an inspiration to get out the door,
to world peace, nation same-speaking peace unto nation,
so charas could criss-cross from Dresden to Dresden,
Burslem to Bialystok,
happy wanderers, buying pots of tea effortlessly,
and explaining the laws of cricket faultlessly
to Russians Germans Poles and Jews,
without an itch and nary a crux word.

6

Is our language complete? No way José
exclamation point. For all the rolling off the tongue
words remain such dullards, their relations obscure.

I – wish – that – she – would – call.
Just tell me, if you can, how what I mean is there.
Or even in: *I – do – wish – that – she – would – call.*
Just tell me, if you can, how what I feel is there.
How do such, or any, sentences give forth,
bring into presence, stand in for, resemble… ?
No way. But just watch them do it.

7

Is our language complete? Are you kidding?
Very often. Which is part of the lack.
I can't claim though that I am lied to often.
Even house-agents' clerks don't say the thing-which-is-not
deliberately, they are just optimists
by training, and the ones I know, the press they get,
it's hard not to sympathise. Would he really
leave a girl like that in her bedsit in her nothings?
Could her executive comportment turn peevish,
lead to murder in the master bedroom even?
I don't know.

8

Is our language complete? You bet it is!
Name one thing it can't do.
It can dawdle meaning-less-ly like this,
or be doing the same thing soul-ful-ly, if it says so,
drifting along the ramparts in a floaty dress,
the chalky hills [*enter here*] in the moonlight,
could be given anything to do,
as they were once said to skip.
The only question it has to ask itself is
how much is a sufficiency, elegant or otherwise?

9

Is our language complete? Well, you read the lines /
lies in the last poem, decide for yourself.
In truth I stumble and cast about even when
I'm talking to myself. There are the best of tools
in the tidiest of racks under the stairs
and these words are not among them, nor – I 'hazard' –
are there any such places words may be found.
But do not despair – and that's an order –
there are no angels, thus no perfect prattling,
and the painstaking repair of spiders' webs
best left to what's best adapted.
As the nightingale 'with her sweet self she wrangles'
we must just strive with our creature tongue.

10

but who can I talk to? To you?
I'm always looking for a way to talk
and I could talk to you
but who might you be?
Are you a parson and should I be afraid?
See! I feel you misunderstand already –
I don't mean these days a reverend
but someone parsonical, already guyed
by the adjective, already gagged
but still mumming in that corner of my eye
I will not turn to –
Oh, you are not my heart's delight,
you load my heart, you want me
for your adversary and that's fair enough
in a democracy, and though I know I would lose
the argument, something I really fear,
what is the most you can deal me,
what would stand me bare-headed in the market place?
I know, but with the lily-stink about me,
not in words, or otherwise, can I turn to you.

11

I'll take me to the *visagiste.*
She won't say, 'Mornin' Squire, how're y' diddlin'
but just set tranquilly to work so that, without a word,
I have every assurance of a new face.
My polpy, and as twilight falls, geranium-coloured nose
will be no more; my skull bones will be cracked
and blended, no longer angular;
my skin – how you say? – hydrated.
Smat! Smat! I shall be new.
I shall know who I am.

12

Things are not what they seem.
This is the big idea of the detective story,
as of Plato. What is really happening as
I study his palm is that the conjuror
has taken my braces and my watch.
There is always a second world
and it's not even out there,
we're just watching the wrong thing.

But in the worst of mysteries there are no clues,
or, if you *must* believe in them, they cannot be read.
Who took my braces, my watch, the lost children may,
the authorities say, never be known,
save in the parallel and smug universe of crimes.

13

No, not suddenly; gradually, bit by bit,
and reluctantly, after much valiant struggle,
one recognises the disorder:
one cupboard, cabinet or tallboy will not do,
place mats are never in their place,
nor tea towels, pillowcases, serviettes;
the crucial kitchen-drawer always has
the wrong batteries, withered elastic bands,
part-warranties, a fuse, sundry string (some plasticated),
a dead pen-torch and none of it helps,
despite planning,
none of it helps –
objects that survive, survive,
like this stout black box 12 inches × 6 × 6.
One must never admit it is all one has.

14

Hotshit philosopher, just tell me *what*
is always veiled, or, at least, you know, the *kind* of thing?
or what on earth are all our interpretations
of?
I'm guessing I'm not to expect
a silver ladder from the parted clouds,
nor a window to open
and she let down her hair.
These are the beautiful stories of revelation and release
and are ruled out.

Yes, in fairness, I know you know
that fewer even of you yourselves
can, or would want to turn your heads towards
– crudely put, but how else? – the truth,
and return to tell us just how things are
and thus should be

– fiercer yet burns the fire,
the shadows ever more spectacular
and Virtue no longer tries to peep
but foxtrots, jogs or saunters in the flames.

15

He'd been waiting for a taxi, Pamuk says.
He had got home at last, and just as he put his key in the lock
he concluded that any meaning anyone might find in the world
he found by chance.

I'm not happy with this.
If the only meaning comes by chance
is chance the only meaning?
But understanding taxis and understanding birds,
earthworms or foxgloves,
following the methods each for each,
might reveal the same algorithm eventually,
and each algorithm slot into the next,
ever outwards until we have some such triumphal cry as

'l'amor che move il sole e l'altre stelle!'
and, before you laugh, if one thing is to move
heaven and earth might it not best be love?
There is a voracity for laws which I know I feel,
just like the man approaching his own front door,
I would conclude, conclude.

16

The beauty outside constantly interrupts.

George Seferis, *Journal*

These black-eyed, snow-white pansies for instance,
careless of their opulence,
generous little souls,
and the raucous lorikeets, green and red,
in the trees near the ocean,
and the ocean and the ocean of light they live in.

I could cultivate an indoor phrase, 'pansy-blind',
as though there is a tale to be told of them
as of every meadow, grove and stream.
Better not interrupt,
which will have to mean: be blind, be deaf,
do not push fingers out towards them.

Can it be true one ancient put his own eyes out
to see more clearly? Can we think yet?

17

Courtesy of Reg Mombassa
I should like to draw attention
to the part-consonance of
Calvary and *Clovelly*.

It is not immaculate, not as nice
as a parallelogram, agreed,
but does serve as a pointer
to what, in language, might sort with what,
what might tumble together
as false friends do
leaving us as under a signpost
which has been tampered with overnight
and is now trying to keep a straight face.

Which leads me to ask have you ever noticed
how the Madonna is always trying
to get some reading done?
The book is falling to the pavement
as the angel calls,
or open on her lap,
or on the lectern
with a book-box spilling over by her foot;
even later on she is still absorbed as the bambino
finds a wicked thorn to play with.

Must she have had some other life,
and, it seems to us moderns, a very modern one,
but it fell away?
Could it be said she was saved from words?

18

Suppose I gave up reading:
wouldn't I start to realise at last
that being genned up on the dispositions
at Caporetto, or the strange under-the-raft world
of poems, or made-up lives
in made-up towns in north Ontario,
or even the best thumbnail cribs of Socrates
are not going to profit me?
What is stock for the mind?
If we can make Nature wordless
is she then not enough?
especially if I choose just one thing to stand for her,
nothing rich like persimmon or lavender
(no sightless pansy or brash lorikeet)
but – a spade-chunk of marl perhaps,
nasturtium-yellow, glinting on its cut side
for a few moments, then lustreless, immobile,
and wormless, but something that might unload
and exalt the mind, and in this way
make it the study for a better life.

19

In the reading rooms for working men,
it was written:
'Get Knowledge, Get Understanding.'
But what I keep thinking is
I don't know what the mind is
other than something
that tries to keep me safe for a while,
without, it seems, being exhausted by the task.

20

But is the breeze my superior?
Yes the mind's a house pressed hard
between two trees, fir-like, dark,
both growing from what they do not know.
But when it thinks '[*dash*] knows'
it knows it means, *de facto*:
'It is known' and remains only to be found
and we can get on to it – hurrah! hurrah!
This is how I keep falling for Progress.

21

Distant percussions. Perhaps a bird-scarer,
perhaps a practised shot practising,
perhaps – though there would first be puffs of smoke –
the detonation of dead fireworks for safety's sake.

The mind can associate anything with anything
and casts about: will sounds go with sights
or movements, this wisp of thistledown going quickly by?

There is probably no end to this ingenuity,
but let's be frugal and not seek for examples.

Today, and maybe for all time, I will insist
that the percussions must also be met elsewhere,
in a space that is more than this mind.

22

To finish a swim, to come back from a walk
as the mist dissolves below,
as the fruit warms on the tree
and to turn to newspapers is,
as George Seferis says,
to rip bandages from miserable wounds.

There is life but not the same life.

23

Sharing air and age and books,

tap-tapping to each other, cy-dots,

but a lizard braves the sunny square
and is faster than a bird's glance to its cleft.
You stumble, one step is more than a thought.

While you wrestle the Beast hourly
I stretch out along a divan and a stool
for twenty minutes' nice shuteye.

How much of life is dancing?

How much of life is movement?

A blink for yes, two blinks for no.

24

Already most upright in his plastic chair,
as the musicians lift their instruments
he lifts his head and fixes the stage steadfastly.
For all we know the music may be something to do tonight,
it may be more of the noise to be endured everywhere,
it may be a gift whose moves and shapes will not numb

but release his mind. For all we know –
that is to say, 'however much we know',
dismissing what we know not as immaterial
but as not sufficient.
Living next to widowhood we are onlookers only.

25

Some simple sights for some states of mind
must be cruel. For the bereaved,
threads of all kinds must tear at the heart –
the wind rips the spider's handiwork
and she rebuilds and rebuilds.
Out of a cleft in the rock
the hand of a fig reaches outwards,
its five flat fingers, clawing for light,
sometimes waving mechanically, like a joke-hand.
Ignorant life it wants, its own kind of hale-and-heartiness.

26

What am I doing here? I do mean here,
doing something *here*. This ant on the page,
it is doing something, maybe trying to get off –
what is there in this snowfield for him after all?
So in that sense doing something,
I feel I ought to be doing when I'm here.

Is there something I can do for you?
Dead six months now and it is unbearable
to think all is discharged –
if my bit of the obsequies was done ok
is that it? Just to say
that what I am doing here is remembering you,
does that join the realm of acts
like giving money and digging wells
even if it's most like grave-tidying,
graves being things made for those who cannot care
for them, or notice them.
Graves, words (even graven words) always misaddressed,
the helplessness of remembering.
Another ant, another purpose for its tentative forefoot.
But I know you would not have me turn away.

27

'— is', is just to say, *that there* is
(the recourse to italics is regrettable,
survival of subject more compromising still)
and is, unpredicated, without profile, pronoun, names
or parts nothing outside, all things gathered in,
by thought and only by thought,
by the kind of mind we are –
and already I have said too much
and am tumbling into instances
as thought just as quickly disaggregates itself
into a day's worth of light,
the belly of an ant,
and other mortal things.

28

Can the universe become, no, I'll rephrase that,
is it – at heart – something like
the motion of bicycle wheels,
nothing of the tubing, leather, chrome, rubber
just the movement
can I ever see just the movement?
just the relay between wheel and wheel?

Is this idea ridiculous?
Is this a dangerous idea?

29

There aren't many poems start this way,
but what I'm flagging is that there is always
something prior, something that has dwindled
or hung out, inexpressible or unspeakable,
some murmur-mutter before the throat-clearing.

So every start is in the smack and dab of things.
The conversation has been up and running so long
when I teeter in from a side road
on my velocipede it seems I can't keep up,
though no one's doing more than looking for clues,
looking at death from this side.

30

remembering the Pack Horse Hotel

Might I yet attain, at 65, with me old age pension,
me own ataraxy? Will I have earned it?
I'll make my case by saying I've never been one
to come on with 'some says one thing, some says another,
and who knows? And what's the odds?
Let's go down the pub.' I've sat in the pub,
and worried away (like Bertrand Russell sat in Whitehall
worrying away) highly engaged in argument,
sloshing beer on the barmaid's feet:
'God is dead. Long live the God that failed!'
'All hail the people's Bomb!' and other burdens.
And latterly, notebooks, full of it, worrying away.
So now, can I let me be?

The cherry tree does not worry away.
For all the ruffling and bending
of the daily wind it sways with calm.
It will not even mind its splintering,
which will come.
It does not even need to say
'Be as I am.'

Yet it is not: that is, it cannot be
in any way that we can think. It will not serve.

Ataraxy – A taxi – A tisket – A tasket –
always   whirr-whirring away

31

A sliver of red floor shows us just where in the room
his figures stand; behind them he paints the dust
hanging in the air. This is the spectacle of the world,
where it is his angels are
in the atomic swirl of an afternoon.
Piero knows that even he does not see everything,
this is just one of many seeings
and without shadow he would be blind.

32

after Gordon Matta Clark

He tears away the wallpaper and there is the street
fifty floors below, the carpet is sucked through the floor,
flapping downwards, snagging on plumbing pipes and ducts.
He exults: nothing is built but falls.
Laminates peel, cement perishes,
reinforcings poke through like fingers, buckle and rust.
Only in distress is art, he says,
Manhattan's coppery cliffs are sliding downwards,
crankshafts, old wheels, the guts of stoves are falling,
the plazas craze and flake into junkyards,
it's all a toy to take to bits.
The artist must not make but see what is hidden,
he says, breathe pure oxygen, what is always hidden,
he says.

33

sacking and gold: *sacco ed oro*

and be assured this is *not* the sun
you're looking at

this painter insists: do not look for the sun

I want my freedom and nothing I make
depends: tar is the stuff it is,
likewise pumice and Cellotex

and freedom must always be
vigilantly guarded

not for me a gas fire
and all that naked, scrotal love.

34

People get married now in aeroplanes
and the Pope has one of his own
and yet the world is still not modern!
Especially art, pottering in poppy fields and corn!

Now, circling over Verona, the arena tilts
this way then that, like a saucer,
so, see, there is no fixed point,
all is in motion and the view from here

'imposes a profound contempt for detail'.
Who cares for that man's tie, her scarf or skirt?
As it has always wished, the spirit soars from the earth,
our sculptures shall be mobile as the clouds,
cities burst upwards like chrysanthemums,
everything is dissolving into art!

35

35–41 after Mario Schifano, painter, 1934–1998

I don't like Nature. I can try to though, and I do.
I look at it and after a while it does become
almost a landscape. There are green patches,
tawny patches, glassy patches,
and squinting I think I can make out
a small school of water-birds,
though they might be the much-relayed reflection
of houses near the shore. Do they move
or do they not? This is what exasperates me –
the anaemia – dots that might be birds' eyes
staring at me. I lose interest.
This grey cat is darker down the spine,
then faintly striped outwards –
But now that's pissed off leaving another blind spot,
another gobbet of it empty and un-understood –
like the two-tone jackdaw's cawing
as it visits and departs the apple tree.

36

The unicyclists on a tightrope are either
going at it *mano a mano* or jiving, it's hard to tell.
I hate Art. I can try not to, and I do, but to me it's like
climbing out through a difficult doorway in the rock
to meet what? Some light?
There might be a Chairman Mao
seen through a venetian blind – could be affecting –
and I am always taken by sand or chalk,
blown, poured or scattered on to adhesive
so that a childhood seems stuck there
in the glints and hillocks, the bits of the alphabet,
a piece of paste costume jewellery,
and now archaeology is necessary, geology even,
for this could be the Cretaceous of a life
I am entering, though it is hard to tell,
and what might be the right slippers or shoes?

37

If, after our ice-cream, we walked up some steps,
went inside and saw a photo of myself,
caught on a very good day, in just the right light
by that beautiful blonde photographer-mistress
(so it's said) to half the Rolling Stones,
blown up on a wall 10 feet high by 20 feet wide
with an invitation to the public to come and worship,
and Lila said 'Was that you, Grandpa?'
what would I make of it?

Did I ever recline just so?
Did I ever really meet a gaze as I met that lens?
And: how much do I love what once I was?

It can seem that I'm still what once I was,
struggling not to sniff, my finger in my eye.
But don't feel sorry, nor pause to imagine
major or minor shames, shallow cruelties
that I pray are now suppressed,
for these are not why I would want to turn away.
That surpasses even embarrassment,
the reason is just there in the steps of passing.

38

Schifano calls this painting 'sulla giusta soluzione
delle contradizioni in seno alla società'
which I will construe thus:
in seno, in the breast – we strike it here –
is where we feel for this as with the rising gorge,
the catch in the throat as we cry 'Justice! Justice!'
and have marched arm in arm;
and *in seno*, deep in the breast, deep in the heart,
wound as I imagine it, like the tightest, most intricate
serpent-coil, or the most intent spool, bobbin, armature,
lie the contradictions:
wealth is poverty but poverty is not wealth.

I would like to make a picture of the *giusta soluzione*
– what would it look like?

39

It will have to start with a line, in a circle,
and inside it I will draw me and mine.
But then the circle must be bigger
so I can accommodate you and yours,
and every detail of me and mine and you and yours
must be in accord so that I do not lavish
my attention on this vest, or that smile of mine, or yours.
But then the circle must be bigger
for the detail requires it and there is no reason
why those who are not me and mine or you and yours
should not be inside with us,
and I must attend to every eyebrow
and this is becoming back-breaking work,
even though all paintings are of something, not of every-
thing.
But perhaps all of us can be symbolised,
say by a perpendicular and even stroke.
And now I can go on,
and the circle is become so wide none is outside
so there is no need of the line, or the stroke.
The picture is perfect. There is nothing there.

40

Space available. As my mind looks around
it sees a good deal: my love,
my great good fortune, my children,
my children's children. Then there is the lake
seen from above and the clouds' footfall upon it,
lifting, vanishing, resuming;
and the lake at my feet by the landing stage
with its arrhythmic slap-slapping
and its secret flowing away into the reeds.
This is not the complete picture of course.
Both lakes I am making stand in,
scribble-shading them to suggest happiness.
And there is, or, *but* there is, space available,
shapeless patches which if they are in the eye
must be in the mind, resolutely empty
of everything: lake-water, children laughing, even clouds.
I think they are the meadows of irreducible despair,
untenanted, but always to be kept aside.

41

quick quick quick quick quick quick quick quick
just the feet quick quick the shoes not court shoes
men's shoes office shoes immaculately laced-up shoes
the trouser turn-ups falling all but to the welt
nothing else visible the foot at its full angle back
each step reiterated quick quick quick quick
you want to join such a step everything

is in such a step the shoes will be shined
leather-soled and heeled not marching steps
not marching feet regular steps regular feet
the world wants to join such a step quick quick
quick quick quick quick quick

42

after Luca Fontana

I've remarked elsewhere on that razor-slash –
bold, vicious, into no more than canvas
but modelling for sure a greater anger
against all that presents, against all surfaces, all faces,
What is behind it? Black black black.

So it is a surprise to meet again
these punctures into the void
and see them now delicately cut,
even affectionately it seems,
small upturned isosceles, and so connected
they seem like lines of bunting,
no red white and blue, nor red white and green,
only grey, chalky white, the smears
of an accidental world and – how can it be? –
the little black flags,
nothing in themselves, but with a slight curl inwards,
are not so much baleful as jaunty.

43

I am I think indifferent to titles
but to be the Professor of Perspective,
how cool would that be!
The said Professor is said to have expired
crawling from his death-bed across the floor
towards the light as it split his shutter.
From the bed he would be in the middle ground,
the sun of course the vanishing point. Or could
the tumult of his sheets just be suggested
and he in the near foreground be reaching
towards where we, spectators, stand,
the light falling flat upon his face.
Given strength the Professor could have shuttled
among all such views as these, indeed chosen
every minute of the cardinal in turn to make a human view.
'The Sun is God,' he cried, but only the sun
sees the death-bed and the cry and everything
in heaven and earth in one single plane.

44

In none of the senses can this be art:
the Highway Surveyor's Department
has been along and spray-painted the roadway
with signs to mean 'dig here'… 'amend'…
'pipe'… and through rain and shine
the codes lie weathering into the many greys
and granulations of asphalt. The road waits.

Until the painter happens by with his Polaroid.
He looks down. A car passes over. He blinks.
He blinks. A van. A bicycle. (For variation.)
He blinks again. They make no difference.
Home with his snaps he takes up his brush
and enters the marks, goes into them,
what other way is there to put it?
He enters the marks.
There is something else in there,
the road-code is a gift,
but there is something else in there
and only his brush can find it out.

45

after James Gleeson

'The Arrival of Implacable Gifts' is,
before it is anything else,
itself a wondrous gift.

Thank you too for your 'Sewing Circle'.
My notes wonder if these women are witches or Bretons,
and whether their dress-trains are trugs or cribs.
There is a child with tiny specs, I spot him.

But what have I missed?
My notes are not your picture.
Is that man being sewn into a tapestry Leonardo?
Near the seashore did I see shells
or peacock feathers, or shells
on peacock feathers?

Through such frail canals does one mind seek another.
The effort is the first thing I thank you for.

46

again after James Gleeson

And then you saw Italy!

Three cypresses and an umbrella pine,
the piazza a seashore where the boy David lies flat,
his head thrown back in a rockpool;
and the Madonna, in a private moment,
her blue gown thrown across her hips,
tends to her hair, and a hennaed girl,
wound in pearls and jewelled flowers,
floats on the waves from Africa.

And Man, who up in those flame-struck forests north
could not be the measure of Nature
but only part of its tumultuousness,
could be this boy in blue jeans,
jacket open, shirtless,
who has just crossed the unseen sound
and now, breaking the perspective,
berths his boat beside the colonnade.

You give me faith, my friend, you give me faith.

47

Grammatical am I, I now realise, am realising,
and since error always comes hard on the heels
of grammar, therefore I am already in error.
It is clear I do not know what I am saying.
I do not know what I am doing.
I do not know what I should do
but nonetheless I should be sure that
(I have heard this now many times)
I am acted and when I am done
I will have been passed through Nature
(a way of putting it I did not make
myself) as through a sentence, parole, parade.

48

'Inside' we say, or 'deep inside',
or '*in* my heart', or 'but with*in*
I feel… the feeling persists'
'in here', and we strike our chest,
'here', he taps his chest, '*sono vecchio*',
this is where I am old,
this is where I was young
in here is where I am.

49

I'm on my way now.

I am at the lights, the crossing, School Lane,
better wait, I can't get these new switchings,
and this new phone.

Past there now. I've crossed over.
By the chip shop, well nearly.

You know I have to stop now.
The bridge is like a hill to me.
Is that how long I'm taking?
I'm doing as best I can.
No, don't fetch me.

Are you late? I'm sorry. Have you loaded the car?
I will be there, but I have lost this street.

I know I live near a tree.

50

for Louie on his third birthday

Think of the crab's outrage when it insists
'I am not a crustacean
I am a crab, and myself.'

Likewise other creatures will not recognise themselves
among those typed by the Emperor;
or those who drink only from a china cup;
or those who once broke the moon.
Remember too the doughty penguin
never in troop with zebras, pandas and their like.

And how outraged are you, three years old today,
when you say 'I am not three, I'm four!'

51

Lucky fuck. That's me I mean. Fucking lucky
every which fucking way. Not a piece of my fucking life,
fucking definitely included, to fucking moan about.
Never fucked over at the proper or improper time
by melancholia, never dropped a buzz-saw
on my fucking leg, never told 'fuck off' by my kids
(fucking kids), no cancer or other fucker's worming
its way through my guts as best I know,
and 'Fuck the rich!' is ok by me 'cos I'm not
one of them, though I mustn't fucking grumble
and I don't, not fucking much.

Fuck me, what a life! Again, ah thanks.
Again? What a jousy and lucky fuck am I,
and I'd better fucking believe it.

52

A solitary walk by a riverside,

or starting early with my dog,

in either case *indulging a reverie*

though I know what *melancholy will attend*

since I would know and do not,

would be acquainted with

the nature and foundation of government, the principles of evil and of moral good, why I approve of one object and disapprove of another, call one thing beautiful and another deform'd? what are truth and falsehood, reason and folly? where am I? by a riverside or not? *or what? from what cause do I derive my existence, and to what condition shall I return? whose favour must I court and whose anger must I dread? what beings surround me and on whom do I have any influence, or who have any influence on me? the cause of these several passions and inclinations which govern me?* what is happiness? *how to decide 'twixt truth and falsehood, reason and folly*

WITHOUT KNOWING UPON WHAT PRINCIPLES I PROCEED

Oh *the dread of error, the absurdity of my reasoning*!
Some smudger with an easel and an oily thumb
can say 'there is nothing that is not a mystery to us',
I must prove Poor Reason. How can I live in mystery?

David Hume answers himself as for himself:

kick back and watch the Test or Tour all afternoon;
eat chocolate; take a front seat upstairs out
to the outskirts, the terminus and back, and back again;
josh with friends; take a glass or three; let reasoning slip
and pay no mind; and dunna worry yooth,
this is Nature helping you.

53

after Georges Rouault

Believing ourselves monarchs,
what follows?

*

Those who put no stock in *maquillage*,
in pencilling, mascara, rouge or gel,
are they the blessed?

*

Those expert in their pencilling
because this is what they love
are they the honest ones?

*

Here's Pierrot in his knickerbocker suit of lights:
'this rich and spangled life
is given to us by life',
but who dares to be a clown?

*

Sometimes it happens that the way is beautiful,
like a single cloud.

*

Tomorrow it will be fine,
said the man clinging to the spar
'without a sight of land'.

*

On the street where you live
the solitary are always passing
and often halt.

*

The nobler the heart
the looser the collar.

*

No one believes
save in his own misery;
no one believes
save in his own deserving.

*

It is a hard horizon:
having been set to living,
at the end harder yet.

*

On your feet, dead men!
Stand up, stand up!

*

dura lex sed lex

54

'Inasmuch as life is *essentially*... injuring... oppressing...'
Ants die between pages, as no doubt in the sweeping of leaves,
and in the Tom Thumb floods of watering the lettuce.
The silhouette on the dyke in the middle distance
has the tread of a man. Were he content
to spend his days picking up stones or leaves,
bunching their stems into small bouquets
would this be a kind of the purest happiness?
There are many we know of, and who are loved,
so turbulent in mind, so injured and injuring
that this is all we can wish for them: life in itself.

55

They are always wise words those
Leonato says to Antonio, both *bravi*,
both old men but still learning the hard way
and Antonio especially willing to give contumely
what for – 'Come Signor Boy!' – and the words are:
'There was never yet philosopher
that could abide the toothache patiently.'

And it is what Melville says among the dunes to Hawthorne,
but then reports how sometimes he can lie on the ground
and feel as though his hair and fingers
are filaments of the grass,
each growing into each so that he knows himself
as part of what he must call the All –
for which there is no sound, not even the least sound.

But then sitting in those sands at Southport,
within the shades of the Customs House,
spear grass poking at the velveteen
and his hat always at risk from the breeze,
the world is back in its old divisions:
Melville and Hawthorne, Antonio and Leonato,
having to make again 'their push at chance and sufferance'
– 'Come Signor Boy, fight!'

56

Melville stretches on the sand.
Did he smoke cigars?
Did he keep a toothpick in his vest?

When he was in his All
what did he get out of it?

Fearlessness? Though not of the kind
born of his love of derring-do –
buccaneer, harpooneer, mountaineer –
but such that, were he picking his teeth of an evening,
leaning on his balcony rail,
and out of the clear sky
lightning found the metal that he held,
and were he granted an instant to think about it,
he would say and mean it: 'Death too is life.
I am absorbed, but nothing is unfinished.'

57

Strike through the mask! Strike through the mask!

Ay, ay Cap'n Ahab.
In some company imperatives are paramount:

Go be a wild man of the woods,
a wild man of the sea,
one of the great renouncers.

There where the mist steams off the hill
is where I want to be.
Let the cloud advance till I am cloud.

58

I hear of other modes of high indifference.

Can I imagine this?
I walk up to my enemy; I slice off my nose.
It lies at his feet. I slice off my left hand.
It drops to the ground. Is there blood in the dust?

Is there pain? If so it is felt.

Who feels it?

This question can't be understood.

Now, how did I intend to do that?

Did I say that I would do it?

By whom would I be understood?

'It was intended' is all that could be said.

But it must be understood.

The understanding is yet more important
than the sharpness of the blade.

There are those who have lived – and died – beyond enigma:
St Lawrence tucking his own gridiron under his arm;
St Agatha, coifed like Freya, imperturbable,
allowing a peek at her bleeding chest,
sometimes her paps held out in a dish;
Karl Liebknecht 'on leave from death'.
These are not more cases of the grand indifference
but some who just knew that this is only the first world,
fretted and sick, and another is, or will be – no matter which –
the good, better, best and real one.

Now, try all that again without
the ambush, be less arch.

It must be possible to tell a story.

A good man cannot be harmed.

The wall plaque reads:

Abitò qui, nel estate 1918,
il Beato Massimiliano Kolbe
che nel lager di Auschwitz
il 14 agosto 1941 offrì la sua vita
per salvare un padre di famiglia

Or in another version:

Here in the summer of 1918
lived the Blessed Massimiliano Kolbe
who in the lager at Auschwitz
on the 14th of August 1941
offered his own life
to save the father of a family.

It must be possible to tell a story.

A Fr. Kolbe (41) a Franciscan
was sent to Auschwitz
by the Germans for sheltering Jews
at his monastery in…

A Fr. Kolbe (41) an anti-Semite,
as his writings show,
was sent to Auschwitz by the Nazis
for sheltering partisans…

A Fr. Kolbe (41) was in Auschwitz
when one man escaped
and ten were picked
to die in his stead…

A Fr. Kolbe (41) was in the line
but not picked out
when one of the ten,
a father…

A Fr. Kolbe (41) heard
one of the men
cry out that he was
the father of a family…

A Fr. Kolbe (41), hearing
one man plead for his life
and his children,
stepped forward in his place…

A Fr. Kolbe (41) who had taken the place
of one Franciszek

Gajowniczek (46), was locked
with nine others…

A Fr. Kolbe (41) who had taken the place
of a Jewish prisoner,
would die
of hunger and thirst…

Saint Max, who is the subject
of my hero project,
led the prayers and singing
and amazed the guards…

Saint Max, who I am
writing about for my project,
lived without any food or water
for three weeks…

One Fr. Kolbe (41), still alive
ten days later when the cell
was needed, was killed
by lethal injection…

Kolbe the anti-Semitic priest
is said to have taken the place of
Franz Gajowniczek
who was not a Jew…

Fr. Kolbe was loved by all
the prisoners, and they reviled
the Jew Gajowniczek
who stood back and survived…

Fr. Kolbe, still alive
when the cell was opened,
offered his arm to the doctor
for the carbolic acid…

Fr. Kolbe was killed
by the usual drug employed,
phenol, injected by the medical staff
straight into the heart…

It must be possible to tell a story.

'Let no man say he is happy until he is dead.'

When Kolbe stepped forward he defeated life,
and he knew he was a happy man.

Perhaps in his summer in Amelia in 1918
he stuck his nose into a dish of tomatoes
just from the stem and right into the stalks
and breathed and smiled and said
'This is life and this is good.'

And then he turned and went through a door
and stopped, as though looking for someone,
and then turned and went out again
and somewhere in this small confusion
put down the fruit and asked himself
'How may the heart be as good as this?
It also lives here.'

No answer spoke. But when he stepped forward
he knew he had learned to let life pass
and was a happy man.

But to be 'the father of a family',
this is life and this is good
and here life cannot pass
and this you clearly knew
as you stepped out to say 'Take me',
or words to that effect, or maybe
'This life is a thing for others.'

You must be understood.

Saint Maximilian Kolbe,
martyr for Charity not the Faith,
and contender for my hero project,
was this your stepping stone
to your better life
when at the last,
having no need of your spectacles,
you will climb naked
and perfectly toned
out of the manhole
the good doctor had
consigned you to,
or did you not see God at all,
only Franciszek Gajowniczek
who was either a Jew
or not a Jew and who cried
'What about my children?'
and who did or did not
do all right out of telling his story later,
and this was all you saw,
Franciszek or Franz, his flesh, his head,
the heads of his children,
and whether or not
you offered up your arm

or let the needle in
'twixt rib and rib,
you are telling me

'Be perfect as I am',
or, as I make you say:
'There is no thing cognisable
that says "Go do thou likewise",
and "A good man cannot be harmed",
there is only a human voice
to say it', as though
I could listen hard enough
to catch it.

59

'We are thus, we know not how.'

The frosted pancreas, even the just-subcutaneous,
harbour sometimes the silliest of worms,
the tiny bestial venoms that are of themselves –
ach! –
no wonder some of us are bound to hate
the snide, treacherous flesh: knuckles too wracked
to write a shopping list,
hate it for the shoes it makes us wear,
the callipers, for its instruction
that you can do nothing but fear
so that you want to say
'I am not this organity,
I am my Rational Soul,

that which is in me and without me
and will be after, or will not be after,
though how can I ever feel
how it had its living formerly
or entered?'

60

This poem is for all those who piss with pain.

But what it is not is a herbal whose good advice
to 'lay the leaves down' (steep them I assume)
should relieve 'them that pysse with payne',
for that must work. I do not offer 'work'.
Art is not a soup from marrow-bones,
afloat with greens, goodness and gratitude.
More humbly, I should say I *cannot* offer 'work'.
So what am I offering? (Art is always offering.)

I'll start with my dishonesty,
that though there was a true dedication (see above),
a call from strength to the sick and unlucky
whose world is next to mine,
as close as the universe of birds
and as separate,
what succeeds is simple selfishness,
the poem's own body trying on its gaudy,

and the call goes astray, thins out,
until they expect less, and less,
and then nothing of me
and my purposes.

61

Quixote's balsam, synthesised to cure every wound and ill,
produces only projectile vomiting
straight into Sancho's beard,
and breeches, pouched and dripping with shit.

Is this the Master's verdict,
not just on all daft worts and roots and spells
but on all remedy, all analgesic even,
for what is to be met along the road?

62

In the modern world, the urinal's periodic belch
brings back to mind the problems of life:
shit-handling in its many aspects;
catarrh in its various modes;
the arts of snot-handling in heavy weather;
flea-flapping; singeing the seams of shirts.

A man crapping,
crouching forwards, shirt-tails in the air,
pants round his skinny ankles,
knees out to open his bowels –
look, there's a levelling line there straight through
from arsehole to 'noble mind'.

But how easy this reduction,
how ready the belly laugh that *shit shit shit*
is this creature's true sum of reason –

how hard to eulogise
the so many Oddfellows,
the Sundays Dad gave for dying Billy Howes,
and those poor dear dead louse-hunters.

63

A man sits on a stool and sings. The people listen.
A butterfly settles on a flower
and someone, me perhaps, must see it,
but this is not the same kind of thing at all.
A man sits on a stool and sings, of love perhaps,
or of jasmine, or acanthus perhaps,
or of cafés deserted in the afternoons,
or of an old man he knew, a character to be sure,
or of a butterfly upon a flower,
and none of these is the same kind of thing as his song.
And the people, me among them, neither are we
the same kind of thing as his song, not at all,
and we listen as he sings.

64

I could get my kicks by dressing well.
I could tax the barber's craft at least fortnightly,
ask more of him than his cut-throat and cologne.
He would advise me on the bandaging
of my moustache and how it might decide
the all-important contour of my upper lip.
A boy's tremor would return to see the taper lit
and approach my nape-hair in his steady hand.

65

So Nature has a hidden order, the philosopher
or cosmologist can reveal. It has a tendency towards
concealment, a disinclination to show its hand
and the skeins of its web are thought all the stronger
half-disclosed, and its whole harmony –
could it be but sprung to view –
therefore shapelier and more certain sure.
Thus we are pinned, half-minds in a half-world
while everything around us is at work,
the banksia, or as it might be, miniature rose,
the near bodiless spider angling,
reflections bending inside bottle-glass.
If I close my eyes what do I see for myself?
a squareish red shadow shimmering in a shirt cuff.

66

I read the world for its hidden order.
In marriage guidance how are J & J
like A & B, and in turn like C & D, or E & F
and what will this yield for happiness?
The misery of such incongruities
haunts the counsellor
who must know cases but cannot seize
even the rough and readiness of cautious laws.
What gets said that destroys a mind for years
will be her province; the titrate of it
is stubborn, inscrutable and cruel.

67

'The hidden order' reprised – it never shows itself
and never goes away.
What? 'We should be content with chance not cause?'
What kind of talk is that?
Item: Doctor, this stuff you gave me –
for the eczema around my eyes?
a new thing to be turning up in my sixty-second year –
does work but it keeps coming back
and I want – sorry – I'd like to know why.
A late-developing latex allergy caught from
swimming goggles seemed very satisfactory,
and readily combatable, if the right ones can be found,
but experiment (no goggles, same rash) nixed that.
I'd like it to be like nicotine, the blue smoke seeps

and wreathes round my fingers and lo!
that sullen, browny, matt-finish yellow,
chemically so well understood.
But this is more like back pain,
except that really is something else:
lying down in a darkened room being fed
grants too much to the thought
that causality requires confusion, order disorder,
predictability – when it will recur – unpredictability.
Nothing hereabouts is really a joke.

68

The hidden *dis*order now, that is never hidden long.
The VAPE Dopopuntura (trademark registered),
works very well on insect bites – it's the ammonia –
but ammonia plus ice and you have
a chemical spill across the motorway,
quickly attended by jokes, confusion's close connivers
for whom skids are always funny, like bites:
Gnasher with a mouthful of trouser,
a bobby bemused by a wasp,
even crocs can be made to grin.
Monotheists convene in Madrid today to discuss
the human tragedy. Monotheists convene today
to discuss the human tragedy in Madrid.
'It's the way you tell 'em,' a hospital spokesman said.

69

Pagliaccio in a rented room, the landlord kindly,
and a tailor has made him an overcoat
of a weight and colour for autumn
and the food downstairs is as much and as good
as he can eat. Yet he bleach-cleans the lavatory
nine times a day, is never at the bidet
less than an hour, the skin round his arse,
the mortician will report,
is as red and rough as turkey-wattle.

Then a good friend seeks him out and they embrace,
laughing at the tears he's felt-tipped on his cheeks
till he again hurls himself on the divan
and his whole body starts and heaves.
Each night, the landlord says, he soft pedals
the piano, singing in his throat
that he is king of all the world,
a world that is new and will yet burst out.

70

In the 1950s when crêpe was new
and people stopped and stared
to watch the Teds slope past Dikiefido's,
the doggies in the window barking and jumping,
we all thought new imaginings of rubber
would change the world –
and plastic then was only just beginning.

71

1965. And thereabouts. Human nature was not
in question: it was good, at heart good,
if 'everywhere in chains', one chain being
'Human Nature' which would have us as
intractable as a fox when with one small
recalibration, tilt or nudge we would be shining.
So are we, in this air and light, almost alive,
or carboniferous, still waiting?

72

Thucydides, what would you say
if you could hear that I am tired,
tired of, don't believe in, broad horizons?
I can gaze all day at a shaftless garden fork,
heavy-brown with rust, useless, probably ugly,
but a thing that cleaves to me, is felt bodily,
as though it brings news
from the very bowels of truth.

Your war, Thucydides, was a very great war,
or it was not. It was complete and reasonable,
or a skirmish in the skirmishing.
What you ask is not that I steady myself
and hold the whole world in my head,
that might have been do-able.
No, what you ask is the understanding of it
once we are past cuticles and oxides.

73

Charlie had too many darlings and too many debts,
upped and went to Canada, not a dicky bird.
Until a card for his mother said he was in Liverpool,
on a troopship just landed. Then, not a dicky bird.

It is the Idea of History to see the categories of time,
and within the Idea are different ideas:
it is all a falling-away, a slow bully-roll downwards;
or it marches, always going up, always becoming, always not
yet.

Charlie and his doxy, up the alleyway by the brewery, act.
Then, still in time, Charlie finds himself at
1st of July 1916, 07.30 hours, up with the lark.
Perhaps. Never a dicky bird.

74

at Kranji War Cemetery, Singapore

'... survives first contact with the enemy'

such as those who came on bicycles
through the jungle
                                        and farewell the *Prince of Wales*
and my Uncle Percy, young blacksmith of Sandford Hill
whose easy sweetness in his photograph
has been with me all my days.

But would that I could have seen him move,
from the kitchen to a chair,
from the coalhouse to the fire;
to have heard him speak,
perhaps just reading the paper –
the loss of what I never knew has been with me
all my days, my mite of the world's wars'
deliverance. But nothing to his mother's,
sectioned for her grief,
locked in all that countryside
until she could say what he is now:
this photo, a frame of ordinary medals,
a stripe of wall, unvisitable,
where he is incised by race,
service-arm, rank, number, and alphabet,
in column 437, everything about him attended to daily
in this needful dream, this phantasm of order.

75

The liberty cap, ah, where did I put it
when I left to drink champagne?
Red as a coxcomb as he wore it
and I admired it,
and called him my *compagno*.

He snatched it from his head
and gave it me and walked on through the arch.
Either it had meant nothing,
an accidental purchase,
or else he knew the game was up

the moth had landed
and nothing strenuous would serve.

I kept it but where did I put it
when I left to drink champagne?

76

Diddle diddle dumpling my son Don
Went to bed with his trousers on,
One shoe off and one shoe on
Diddle diddle dumpling my son Don.

The Flagellator has one shoe off and one shoe on.
Is that for purchase as he lays into his work,
golf-swinging the scourge into enemy flesh,
or is it from a slip and stumble mishandling
the man to the whipping post?

Oh silly Don, as your mother sang,
struggling to learn your shoes,
going to bed with your trousers on – though you never –
and here you are again, one shoe off and one shoe on,
diddle diddle dumpling…

77

The Flagellator, though once a baby
will never be depicted with a baby face.
Snag-toothed always, carbuncled,
no one ever loves a torturer,
not even one of our own.

And this is how we explain ourselves:
History gets him from his mother's lap,
where he implores and fits this to that,
and carves his education in the crafts of pain.
There is this actual world awaits,
its grammar is fixed and carries us to the end,
though itself it has no end,
and so are we absolved.

78

Swimming is the answer, notwithstanding Chairman Mao.
There, that strikes an attitude. What on earth
do I mean? Well, if water ever was our element
it is no longer, yet its foreignness feels welcoming.
It is the sense of suspension and of clothing
at its simplest and most complete.
Admittedly it is escape, nothing to do with here above
except for drawing off the empty air – and maybe
it is blameworthy to embrace such muffling,
such coddling, which brings me on to Chairman Mao,
the Great Unmuffler, Pilot of Reality
for whom the world was full of answers,

one such that swimming is resurrection:
'You thought me dead? Look, seven miles
down the Yangtse, pick the bones out of that.'
But was he swimming or did he just float downstream?
Was that indeed his head singing? Hence the 'notwithstanding',
that and the bones.

79

How much impartiality should we try for?
We look up for an answer? Up.
Down. Straight ahead.
The floaters are stirred up
like the flakes in a snow-globe
Blackpool tower in a white-out.
Blink. Blink and blink again.
Slowly it settles and the viewing platform
returns to view.

And somewhere everything is understood.
Up there – that is the old idea, as frescoed,
and this is the new idea:
the hot news from the ice-cores;
the definitive history
of the Hong Kong and Shanghai Banking Corporation;
every lairage docket ever filed.
These are what move me hither and thither, impartially.

80

I meditate before a smeary window now,
dried rivulets between the panes,
small moraines where the runnels halted,
not quite randomised.

Apparently it can be known who I am
by the particular way I sneeze.

81

Like with a sermon in a high wind
it becomes uncertain who is speaking to whom.
My friends, I am doing my best to find
what it is I have to say,
but I end up shrugging at the street corner.

Of course others will break in,
and so they should, they have every appearance
of entitlement.
Others will be murmuring together,
as though making some necessary plan
and are clustered across the road, heads together,
glancing over their shoulders
and something of what they say carries here.

82

Lady, he does not like your briefcase or your shoes,
nor for certain the London train,
it is all 'darksome clay' to him,
denizen of the underpass,
who must like its wet floor, dark stones,
who must hate all things white, even if they are
'least complicated', 'easiest to understand'
'most pure':

No hurry Lady, clicky-clacky, clicky-clacky
There is no fuckin' place to go
We're only going to the crem.

83

The soul, I'm finding, turns out very useful.
If we have just the world as it is to go on,
how it wags, or its history seen
from any partiality whatsoever,
we'd think *è fango il mondo*,
what a shithole!

But in the dimple, mortise, sinus or grot
that gets called 'soul',
which is always *in in in*,
is, for instance, what gets called 'justice'.
Out here she can barely dress herself, go out
and be recognised – and she must be recognised

and face down those who say
'Who are you?' or 'Where have you ever been?'
or 'We have long forgotten you, we do pretty much
what we like', and she must skulk and bide
and her place of biding in this meanwhile,
this useful soul.

84

Meanwhile, a challenge: find me one person
in any bus queue, or indeed anywhere
who will deny that there's injustice
in this whole wide world of freedoms
and indulgences. Not one. I thought so.
The queue smiles ruefully and soldiers on.
So, Justice, how are you forgotten?
How are you whittled and distracted?

85

Philosophers, divines, all you addicts of good news,
sweet or sweating on the Ideal Power,
you will insist Injustice sits only on a paper throne
forever jumping and starting fearful of a spark,
spooked by a wall, a shadow, a creaking door.
In that case where is the ghost?
I cannot see the ghost.

86

Judge of the world am I. *La vita è bella*
or *la vita è brutta*? It's for me to decide.
Which network and which payment-plan?
Cool. How should I set to work?
The task is to gather up for contemplation
and assize every hair that will testify
to the joy and beauty of the life
we mortals lead, then put in litigation
every smudge upon the scene.
The rules of evidence must ban the ping-pong
of examples, smiley faces versus amputees.
Synechdoche is opportunist, often cruel.
Ciao bella. Ciao brutta. The court will rise.

87

In portraiture, what I favour for myself
is that nineteenth-into-twentieth-century
seaside look. *A bas* the aldermanic,
fists closed over the lion-carved chair-arms,
calf-bound History and Law behind,
frozen for the flash.
I want something more *Le Touquet Plage*,
dashed off, *impressioniste*, as though my laughing mistress
is just out of frame or shot and I am eager
to be off. Or even the style of collier lads

on the Isle of Man with their canes, boaters
and blazers plucked from the props box.
Not that I despise the aldermen who build and serve –
but oh, white sand, white flannels, something sunshiny.

88

Generous as it is, loving indeed to many,
the mathematics cannot help. There's a bumble-buzz
from the listening devices but nothing parsable;
from the ooze the odd statuette
brought up with the abalone is not germane;
naught from the geological squires;
nothing even from Darwin's beloved stenches.
For all-of-it-together, common-or-garden
taken-for-granted Being, for the universe –
whatever that is – nothing speaks.

So we are left to our own intricacies,
gli animali parlanti, the speaking clocks,
yapping at the Giant's castanets
like dogs to a bagpipe,
some of us stomped, some of us squeaking free
only to fall into allegories like this of
Human Ignorance where *Virtus Humana*, poor lamb,
has changed herself into a tree
she's that pissed off, and there we all are
down in the *fosse*, the pit, the maggot tin
and there's only Hermes (why Hermes?)
lending a hand to grasp and pull by one arm – who? –

Some who might yet try to find joy in the found,
like Whitman on his walks smiling at every sparrow,
though now bits of metal, half-beams,
rope both whole and unstrung, human things,
pieces that can be drop-soldered into non-machines,
tiny or bus-sized with such elaborate juncturing
and levering. Meanwhile the patient louse
ports its carapace across the speckled stone.
It is no model though, and no way to end,
not even this part of the conversation.

89

Like many others of my ilk this is not something
I like to talk about, but since, despite everything,
it still makes sense to talk of –
oh, wait, in my notes 'talk' is crossed out
and replaced by 'think' –
since it still makes sense to think of G—d
(as my religious students always write it)
especially, as I now have a philosopher's warrant
that s/he could be described by any analogy,
anything could be slotted into the sentence –
'father' (usually) 'watchmaker' (several times), 'spider'
or 'A' 'AA' or 'AAA', Adidas, *ad infinitum*,
it still makes sense because something must go just there
in such sentences that we do need like:
' — knows', ' — is good', ' — is just'
' — watches', ' — loves (me)', ' — is'.

90

So, I say *so*, if what G—d is is an unavoidable way of talking:
when everything has been imagined,
at least until everything is spoken whereof we cannot speak –
how many such sentences should we try for?

'G—d knows' let us take; and unpack:

day
Should lose his light when men do lose their shames,
Betray their cause of being

'G—d knows' *our cause of being* which is:

since we have a brain of a kind

can recognise the shapes and some shadows

of this world, in other words we can think –

G—d knows we can think! –

our cause is to think together,

one of another, and that must secure us here

and then comfort us somehow.

So, a first sentence can be: G—d loves Reason.

91

On my veranda I have to imagine more.
Sometimes, even on an easy day, it is difficult;
sometimes things can come unbidden, as they should:
a calabash of babies' hands rests in the hearth,
the little amputees themselves are who knows where.

Will it help to study more? Certainly.
And we have sought fore and aft, hither and yon,
up hill and down dale – we human things will not rest
until we know that the peace is within us
as once it was, and unabashed as once it was –
we *must* return. Or we might be new,
straightened at least, even refigured,
not quickly, but as we shall need to be.

92

I am always on the lookout for routines
and perhaps I can make another out of what I'm doing now.
I have woken early and stayed put.
Behind the shutters it is dark so what we call the day
is beginning only in noises: birdsong obviously,
which is at present an eight-call sequence
gargling in a pigeon's throat; other note-rows are
too fast to count. There are trees in a light wind,
a thousand leaves perhaps, and I realise
I have never thought to wonder how many leaves
a given tree might carry on a given day –

not a routine. A car starts and idles,
the driver checks her bag for tissues and for keys,
and further off – light is coming in now – a dull then whining pitch
resolves itself into a wood-saw. Whoever works it,
already stripped to the waist, is properly guarded I hope,
and alert. And little of this, really, is what I hear,
and what would the routine accomplish? Haphazard
attention? Exercise for the inner eye?
Let it be itself (reason enough for routines?)
A wasp is buzzing by the wall.
There are, I'm convinced again, surrounding worlds.

93

A lawyer on the beach,
jacketless, but still with my thin bow tie
in place, my pencil-moustache not yet
glistening and though my nose is reddening
I look straight at you, the viewer,
client, adversary – whoever you are.
'The nobler the heart the looser the collar'?
No, I don't entertain that.
Over my right shoulder a noonday light
is merging my shirt and the empty sand,
my outline is becoming all but lost.
Will this make you warm to me?
I feel sure in my eye there is a twinkle to be seen.

94

May the barber find happiness with his bearded lady.
May the wife who found her husband hanging
and tried to cut him down find a good companion
and stroll and kiss in the starlight.
May the slow one, the lame one, the ugly one
always be as welcome among the girls.
May she who never rests, who walks in the same street
all day every day with just a cigarette, find rest.
May she who grieves – he left after lunch,
at 3 he lay crushed in the field –
smile at one small thing and at length at another.
May there be dancing in the piazza!
May there be fruit upon the vine (literally).
For this is not a wicked but a hard world,
and people struggle, without a scheme of things,
and deserve release. That's it, willing it so.

95

There is the world we die in and there is nothing.
The shades know this, hence their clamouring,
which we learn to turn from, and which fades away.
Despite appearances, the gardens of remembrance
are full of resignation. 'At rest', they rest.
We stop by but are ushered on our way.
If we did not act as though this were true
what would become of us?

*

There is the world we die in and there is
somewhere we cannot visit, still less lodge in,
and we call it Truth.
(Do not be embarrassed to name it;
the hostess is a worthy lady
of impeccable, that is to say of course
no parentage, nude and desirable,
nude and pure as the sky, though, in a word, untouchable.)
If we did not act as though this were true
what would become of us?

WHAT MUST HAPPEN

'Funny – to be a Century –
And see the People – going by –'
EMILY DICKINSON

1.

Now all the Sciences of History are at the door,
The World's Reason and his suite,
Long-stirruped, rearing, riding,
Storming the earth and stunning the air.

Look at His Highness there in white and gold,
And this other in his oh-so-modest blue;
Look how their men are drawn to breast the rise –
Accoutred and alive, how historical they are!

The ensign posts away, along the line, along the day,
And at its end happens upon His Majesty,
Sniffling upon a log, and tip-toes on his way.
Two Emperors can be caught with just one bean.

2.

Now all the Sciences of History are at the door
With caps in hand and aprons spread
Crossing themselves and speaking French.
Small fires seize picture frames and chairs.

In *bibliothèque*, café, *platz* and upper room
Prophets and thinkers sniff the visionary smoke,
Number their theses and dress to kill.
Their aeropainting will re-touch the dawn,

Their willing corporals stun and storm,
Their strapped-up martyrs charge and call:
'Fools, did we think we should live forever?
Look how historical the future is!'

3.

Now all the Sciences of History are at the door
And, after a little stun and storm, shock and awe,
Are smiling, shirt-sleeved, making nice: 'May we come in,
May we sit down? Look at our invisible hands –

The latest manicure! – how may they work for you?
We aim to make the world to count
In perfect synchrony, to teach the world to chant:
"There is no past, all things are new, we act: we are."

So just sign where it says: "In none we trust",
And here again, "In none we trust",
And just once more "In none we trust".
How historical you were, and now how free!'

4.

Now all the Sciences of History are at the door
Or tent-flap, fly-screen, wire-entanglement
And peer in. Still on their jotters there's little spilt
Or spattered, and still they will reiterate:

'Time must be History, and History an Idea
Patient of its uncoiling
To an End. Otherwise we fall through,
Like light through glass, nothing now and nothing then.'

Boys on their cots think they hear water
And the clink of tin: in their dreams of whiskers
They will soon be shaved. Wounds get stuck with cat
Or blanket-hair. What must happen, what need not?

CROCKERY

ANTIQUARIUM

He chomps their squirming comrades one in either hand,
but Ulysses gets the Cyclops drunk, lops and sharpens
a mighty pine, has four men lift it and in lock-step drive it
... but this is a story you know well enough,

like Ulysses clinging to the ram's belly-fleece,
his toes cinched on the creature's balls and seeming to wink
as he slips by the monster's blinded hands.
But why would anyone want these scenes on a water jar?

Perhaps it's meant to show monstrosity worsted by human nous,
gross voracity outwitted by such as cherish table-ware,
cups and plates, things to hold our water, light and wine,
an arm of the technic that helps us weaklings on our way.

All of it will break in time but it will not rot.
Thus a patient girl with a brush and glue
can find us as we were and – we *can* come this far –
weep for Polyphemus and his bleeding eye.

ETRURIA HALL

Wedgwood would not put such pain on his own Etruscan ware.
None of his artists was invited in to capture him,
woozy but upright in his chair as he watched Dr Bent
saw through the thickened bone below his knee.

That goes under 'breakages', along with misbegotten
cream-ware he will not back-stamp with his name
but grinds beneath his wooden heel. Hithering and thithering,
mithering on *bucchero* and what art should grace

my lady's table and Portland pots and salesmanship,
he pegs it back by moonlight to Etruria Hall,
his mind turning on the cogs of betterment as he goes,
fresh glazes, firings and the smooth runnings of his new canal.

From the clay-end to St Martin's Lane everything is canalised:
the mould-maker, pugman, dipper, paintress, gilder, fireman,
sagger-maker, placer, drawer, all in work,
all provided for in New Etruria's commodious light.

DIRT

Window-nets are tell-tales. Idleness will not survive
the war with dirt. So she's on her hands and knees
to stone the doorstep, then the window-sill;
the sweeping of your bricks shows you what you are.

Dust slides in unseen onto mantelpiece and rug.
Collars starched for Sunday-best are smirched by noon –
wash your neck, wash your neck – dolly-peg and mangle
until at last the liberations of Electrolux.

Deep-breathing by an open window, sanatorium-style,
is recommended, but dirt still settles in the phlegm,
bronchitic thickenings, spitting in the street, the scourings
of flint and soft soot pocketed by the hapless lung.

The paintress of majolica licked her brush and died.
Dippers lined their guts with milk and Epsom salts
to no avail. God bless the Factory Acts
that saved my mother from the leaded glaze!

CHINA CABINET

The most delicate of porcelain is made by angry fire.
The magma of manufactory, Vesuvial spits, globs and drops,
imitating how the earth made itself
from a belly of entombed or tunnelled flame.

And it creates this wasp-waisted girl in crinolines,
cheeks just ablush, slim fingers offering a posy
of forget-me-nots for their ceramic scent,
her slipper cool enough to step on ice.

Soon she shall have her spaniel and her swain,
Jemima Puddleduck and Mr Fox for company,
he in knee-breeches and frock coat, hands behind his back
looking most lawyerly as he inclines to listen in.

This is her domain where she can breathe air
as un-flecked as her gown. Live here my lady,
safe from all that muck outside:
you are the beauty we have come to know.

HOMUS ECONOMICUS

And thousands of 'em sold, these gentle and
respectful maids, their blushes packed in straw,
all entrusted to the slow canals, just as Etruscan potters
sent their stuff down the Tiber to the mouth of Rome.

Homus economicus, dragging from the local quag
a tea-service to Queen Charlotte's taste;
mollifying 'fat housewives' who want their ware
more or less 'yallower Mr Wagwood, *if you will.*'

'Stout classicist', entrepreneur of grave-goods,
always testing novelty: black figure, red figure,
Venus modelled against a choice of blue, black, lilac,
sage-green or any manganese that can be found.

Then he's liberation's honourable fashionista:
his medallion of the kneeling slave in jasper-ware –
'*Am I not a man and a brother?*' – soon *à la mode*
as tea-caddies, hair-pins, bracelets. Thousands of 'em sold.

GOING GLOBAL

Smithereened along with Royal Art,
I doubt our old cow-butter can be found
among the world's new earthenware. China
comes from China, as it may, my lady from Brazil.

Like them, our folk left the one-egg farms for work.
Now, as then, cities grow like marrows in the wet:
shanties and dormitories rigged, showrooms lacquered.
Backache. Repeat. Silica. Repeat. Breathing. Repeat.

Breathing... Do they do this better than was managed then?
In infant death for instance: Longton
in 1899 – 327 per 1000.
And how many years are the median now? > 46? < ?

The analysts don't count this up. They seek the shortest way
and watch the money blink across the globe.
It comes home safe, folded many times,
and seems somehow to wink when passing by.

THE PRIMS

Here the helpless, hapless, feckless commonage
in congregation on a May weekend at Mow Cop
to hear Hugh Bourne, who, even when speaking to thousands,
could not help but hold a shy hand before his face.

He carts the gospel from place to place, the word
of some god who is not Mammon and who likes the meek.
Who shall inherit. Inherit what? This show below?
potbanks, coal-smoke, salt-fogs, pit-heaps, saffrucks, soot?

These 'dear peculiar people' are not that daft.
They do not expect owt builded here to go up quick.
All they ask, free and familiar, is how to be
a worthy soul, and that their works shall follow them.

Thus Hon Treas., always in his best on Sundays,
rattles year by year his tin of cooperation.
It will add up, even though only copper, into a benefit,
a grand word and a grand thing: all do give so all may live.

Thus Hon Sec. reads the notices for the week, the rotas
and the tasks of patience. She knows that 'e'en the smallest thing
can do some good and comfort bring' and will keep at it,
entering in the minute-book the measures of their joy.

They gave their mite, these ranting Primitives,
a-shivering and a-shaking (agitating!) all through Sunday night.
Filled from the loving-cup, they descend lit-up into the dark.
May those who mock thee learn the dignity of love.

MANCHUKUO

1.

In a garden in Sawtell,
a black butterfly, gold-tipped,
jinks along a line of trees,
over the ferns and on
among the paper-barks.
On the creek two ducks appear
and disappear; purple blooms
waver in the stream
as though on strings;
the house-shadows
adjust their geometries.
By this time the creek
will be moving seaward –
will be, as that fly,
in the same divisible time
as the whip-bird's shout,
stands on the rim of a glass,
the water-dragon
takes a step,
and we carry forwards
what we have.

2.

What do I carry now
of Sandford Hill?
(*Local pronunc.* Sanfa-dill.)
I am trying.
Gaps of memory seem
another failing,

even another guilt.
There is the arch
leading into the old cartway,
the backs with their rough cobbles.
I can't remember its
leading anywhere,
nor where my mind went
in those child-hours
of afternoons out there,
under the arch,
by a few yards of wall,
a few flights of brick,
each brick nose to nose,
a different oblong:
this one wafering
revealing its inmost tangerine,
still a lick of whitewash
about another, several soot-veined,
each one's abrasion different
to the heel of a hand
as I seek the unseen glow
of the baker's wall,
warm from the morning
and still proffered, as,
outside the arch,
the day tightens and withdraws.

3.

The true date
of the start of World War II,
this historian says,
was September 18th 1931.
This was the day
the Empire of Japan,
in becoming the Empire
to vanquish Empires,
invaded / liberated
Manchuria / Manchukuo.

Is the historian right or wrong?
I do not know.
I do know that there,
in the grandeur of time,
someone was sitting in a garden,
someone was gazing at a wall
and were caught up,
made a part, fitted in,
and I think we should try
to understand the flow, the sweep –

Perce, my uncle,
who died of that war,
in some moment of that day,
September 18th 1931,
almost surely,
passed under the arch,
perhaps brushed his coat-shoulder
against the brick

as he swung out into the street.
I imagine him 'swinging'
because he was only ever young
and I have little else to go on,
little to describe,
though I can invent whistling,
boys whistled then.

And as he 'swung out' the last time,
brushing his greatcoat
against the brick,
his kitbag on that shoulder,
perhaps he put his hand to the wall –

But this is harder to research
than the Nine Powers Treaty
the Peace of Paris,
the Washington Conference,
the League of Nations,
the Kwantung Army…

Like those of other polities,
Perce was moving seaward,
carrying forward what he had,
past the arch,
through places –
Malaya, Malacca –
I might just imagine,
to a moment which,
with nothing to go on,
I can neither know
nor conjure.

SUNDAY AFTERNOON

Will Heath, never good on his feet,
turned the corner from Chapel
one smokeless Sunday afternoon,
tippling a little, unjustly, as though
his Sabbath boots were welted with the weekday clay,
and, though always slower still of speech,
often malapropic, was eager with words for me.
He smiled and put forth both his hands.
'Look thee,' he said, and on one palm he held
a box of fire-brick and within it a nest of flame,
and in the other hand a jug, of yellow earthenware,
filled with water to the brim.
'What hast thou got there?' I asked him.

'Look, this is the fire,' he said, 'that can burn Paradise,
and this the water to douse the flames of Hell.
Then all on us will love the Lord
not for our reward, and not for fear on Him,
but for His Own Sake.'

I love thee Will Heath,
but fled the one Sunday afternoon
I did spend in your Sunday School,
put there that through the tall, colourless windows
faith might strike the child.
On the cold bench, odorous with wax and incorrupt,
I sat unstultified,
not lifted up by the pure and empty light,
nor by the men bellowing at hymns,

released as they were from something,
their sins they would say, the father's strap still lingering,
released as they were and recognized –

I love thee Will Heath
and sorrow too for your long, patient widowhood
spent by the kitchen table,
the oilcloth always well wiped down;
your every place of worship closed one by one,
even the red tin tabernacle on worthless ground,
till you were homeless.

And if I met you again in the street,
or cutting across the waste, or wherever,
I would stop you for sure and ask you
how it went with the water and the fire,
and I would hope you would say: 'They are consumed.'
And then I would ask that you take me and show me
the dwelling of such selflessness and unassuming,
and this Lord that you have made.

AGRICOLA

agricola: a word
like shards
cutting the palm,
pieces of the stone sun
re-made in travertine

*

agricola: a response,
a riposte to the earth,
human work

*

much to do with beating:
the near-off clash
of wood and metal,
a knot struck,
the spittle of
hammer-flaw

*

a fork
in the curved track
that keeps on curving,
the widening space between
fitted up with jottings
of bushes and small trees
before the strange wood
and its deep trees

*

all morning
traction through vetches
and horse-corn, once bull-dragged;
at length some polished furrows

*

tanks in fields
for water or fuel oil;
other containers
improvised,
white bath tubs
with tide-lines,
phosphoric green

*

banished machinery,
clustered, rusting together,
better than gawky
some loaders heron-like

*

harrows untoothed,
ploughshares broken on stone
will not go unvisited;
the tinkerers come here daily
to seek a strut, bolt or chain
to use or save

*

in his pound
the sculptor Smith kept a troop of
old spaders, ridgers,
wagons, winnowers
to climb among, dismember,
and then hammer
to something new

*

corrosion:
barrel-hoops,
a garden fork, prongs only,
a mattock head
shaped like a face

*

grease for
bolts and hinges,
malt-brown with
white peaks standing
as the fingers leave it

*

a bunch
of lavender is drying,
hung like a totem sheaf

*

the shed,
its oils, creosote,
dust-gloves, raffia,
nail-box, screw-box,
the rake, the fork, the spade

*

those bloody
nasturtiums in the
cinder-soil
untidy and ungrowing

*

scratty fruit-canes
gone wild, dens and scabs,
coltsfoot is nearly pretty;
fustian dock good medicine
bound on to nettle stings

*

the road to
Rhayader logged
then mined long ago;
the grey spoil-screes,
the head-gear,
its red flaking slowly
into the air

*

hammering again,
now further off;
something is being changed

*

a hot afternoon
and a low ceiling,
a brown strip of paper
uncurling downwards
weighted with flies;
the strange fleecy peach
offered as a treat

*

stench of fern-coverts,
rabbit-droppings look
like currants;
fern-days of purposeless
hiding

*

waste-ground,
whatever margins and
fents of land not built on,
sometimes pasture
for a rag-and-bone piebald

*

on one side
rough grass too steep,
on the other
coal-scree
useless slack
and rubble

*

further round
more spoil, the saffruck,
white crocks
underfoot, sliding
this way and that

*

Agricola
marches upon
the Black Hills
and the Lion's Head;
comes home
'black as the road',
the enemy, unengaged,
'melted away'

*

across the waste,
Peter off the lead
and at once about
the stubborn grasses
the scratched tilth
of clinker and potsherds

*

grasses torn off
for the clay beneath,
white and sopping,
draining on to lorry wheels
spattling the roadway

*

pigeon lofts
furnished from wardrobes,
cupboard sides and shelves,
the fowl roosting

among cup-hooks,
job-lot paint stripes
to bring the birds home

*

old tank containers
sheared down at the corners
and unfolded
like a blown tulip

*

other lean-tos,
a cross-and-bible door
laid on its side,
blue-grey corrugated,
its bolt-holes black or rust-fringed

*

by the gate
tied with orange twine,
the deep-pocketed sludge
under the beasts' feet

*

besides the rough-tough cabbage
hefty potatoes
and bantams scratching,
a farm of coal-picking
and even mining, the seams
slanted into the hill

*

the last tak'in of the fell
yielded winter pasture
though stumbling ground;
the grey-white, pieced
and mounded walls
loosen, the falls strung with wire,
some trodden down of course

*

lawns obligatory:
the seeded area
with criss-cross hairs
fluttering with foil
and rags to serve
against birds,
like a pair of trousers
flap-hanging in a tree

*

lawns obligatory:
swiss-roll turves
with all herbage pared
and relaid –
it's the smart answer

*

aubretia
on its rocky islets
of broken quartz,
cascades white and purple
by front paths and drives,

always much admired
of a summer Sunday
at eventide

*

how well
can be known
an unmade road:
the quartz grains,
cinder glints,
the dull shine of tar-lumps,
each rain-puddle
re-finding its old shape
and depth

*

canal-making
with a beat-up soup spoon
tarnished yellow
but serviceable,
small dams and atolls

*

verandas
always in peril
creepers waving to get hold;
saplings urged upwards

*

the small plum
was split and leans
helplessly; just in
this light, this morning,
its fruit, known
to be purple
is nearly as white
as the stones

*

a quarry
as though one hand
has opened the earth
so talc can be
trundled away
and golden gravel
sieved and washed

*

Agricola: the earth scratched
for a living

THESE THINGS

'But Nature is a stranger yet'
EMILY DICKINSON

Flowers that do not look brisk –
sharp, upright, attentive –
but are always unkempt, dishevelled,
whether in spring-yellow or mourning purples,
seemingly fatigued, distracted,
they care not, but get on as well as better.

And these other creatures at their work,
fond marigolds, that strangely pinkish tree,
a long list of insects, never reposeful,
a bird staying hidden, its song inscrutable,
none of these things is singing or smiling our way.

*

Here, by a complicated tree,
among a few stones, that, as ever,
gaze only at the ground, I am on watch.
Two bright flowers are splashed nearby,
otherwise all is green – or greens –
save the grey tatters of the tree-bark.
A magpie introduces his black and white
and swaggers it around.

Green, grey, black, white,
not much 'claptrap of colour' here.

*

The creek is slowing as it draws to turn.
A tree, grown out over the water
has taken its chance to head upward for the light.
Like the wind, light makes its own alterations
and is different again from the waters'
punctual beck and call.

This much is going on, as we say,
or whether we say it or not.
What is this business of saying?
(It is time I could say something.)

*

Rain today. It brings its own changes:
the bark is darkened, there are glints on leaves,
the creek is spattered.

Below the notch in the tree,
the grey in the bark now looks like tar
clawed downwards across the pale ground.

Heedless, even nerveless, the bush-turkey
checks back and forth across his ground,
his gold throat shuttling up and down.

Warm enough now, the cicadas give tongue,
and a lizard is out on a branch,
monument-still for an hour,
silvery and green. Smart as paint he is.

*

Leaves on the creek demonstrate its flow.
They are like a small fleet, each moving
as though seeking station for convoy onwards.

Then there is the current itself to be seen
ridging the water.
It quickens and then canters inland,
carrying the correct volume and movement for the day
as though it understands itself.

I am on watch.
What might drop from the roof?

*

A sudden whistling in my ear,
a jasmine star with its five points,
the clank of a workman's tools dropped,
the sweepings of the pavement,
leaves and the clatter of leaves,
the rose, upright, noble,
the faint tracery of a tall grass.

I am not going far for these –
I can look, listen and find them.
They seem to be things that I know.

My ear whistles at me,
the five hearts of the jasmine flower,
the brief shout of metal on paving stone,
leaves and litter blown together
and swept across to be shovelled,
the rose also inclined,
the fawn grass melting away.

I am attending
but they are what they seem to be,
as Fernando said
(not his real name).

*

(Elsewhere)

Walking the beach, the wind at our back,
sand-skim rushes before us,
it twirls and eddies,
more erratic than a flock or shoal,
though doubtless there is a rule.

Undisturbed yet, the casts of sand-crabs,
patterned like chase-work,
each copiously and differently done,
might be said to decorate the scene,
each tight drill downwards casually enhanced.

*

I am on watch.
I stoop to the ground:
there is no echo of itself.

There are these things and sometimes the shadow of these
things
but they will not be seen apart.

The pansies in their two colours at my feet –
two purples – keep themselves to themselves.

All I see is time and what might be like and like,
the watch-winding cicadas for instance.
I fear these things are no more than they appear to be.

PREDICTABLE DAYS

If the day predicted falls out
as it should and the small hawk
arrives on its noonday
draft of air and works lazily

across the hill,
and the wind rises in the afternoon,
and the white rock clings
to the light deep into dusk

then time will have passed,
some time will have passed,
and no offence taken,
only its customary tribute.

I like predictable days,
baffled by no more than a sun dapple.
Mystery, the glamorous chaos-engine,
breaks things, lives included.

PASSING

The scrape of a spade
on a paving stone.
An arena of light
on the yellow grass.

The spade keeps working –
something is being made.
The arena widens
as the shadows retire.

It's all change and change-about,
coming and going,
a distant hammering takes up,
then a mattock at the ground, *tac tac*.

I'm feeling carried along –
will nothing pause?
Can nothing arrest itself?
Can no one see this passing?

SHADING IN

A sea-fret might be shaded in,
but then, the sun,
as though uncovering a tureen,
has it vanish quite away.

Vanish – though such a fret can return
stealing . . . but what is it stealing?
It is not furtive, or embarrassed,
it simply shows itself

without any purpose –
it cannot be said to know purpose.
But I cannot let it just
show itself: I must nail and nail,

making it, for example, into a salute…
And the line ends just there.
That tureen now,
was it patterned or was it plain?

SELF-PORTRAIT

after R. B. Kitaj

Did you laugh so, so late?
Was your beard so red, so long?
Were you by then, or always, a Dodgers fan,
or is that cap a prop just come to hand?

By what right do I ask you these things?
And use 'you' so familiarly,
you whom I never met
or even saw or heard, in the flesh?

Is it because one feels one can take liberties
with the dead, as with the slightly famous
who can be papped in supermarkets
or accosted in the common street?

Are self-portraits everyone's property?
have you given yourself up to one and all,
and all who look are worthy
and free to take what they want?

I want that blue cap and orangutan beard,
things I think I can get away with
in this mood for picture-making.
Should you have been so generous?

AN EMPTY STREET

after Ottone Rosai, via San Leonardo

What is there to an empty street?
And one so commonplace,
narrow, with two high walls,
bending out of view.
No one in sight
and no one expected.
No Dame Trot for sure,
with her basket over her arm,
the check cloth covering dainties,
her hat perched so,
her pince-nez expectant.
Even she has hurried away.

*

What is there to an empty street?
The photo (bottom right,
curated later)
shows the doorway
to have been your studio
(there's a plaque).
Still no one to see.
Have they tiptoed round
another way, anxious
to preserve its vacancy for you
and leave your lines,
so carefully set forth, intact?

*

What is there to an empty street?
Let's get impatient,
let's add a soundtrack
somewhere beyond
but coming on this way.
We'll have a marching band,
cornets, clarinet
and big bass drum,
at least the air is moving!
Until we lose control –
the band has wheeled away.
You, or the street, has won again.

*

What is there to an empty street?
Have you seized it
for your melancholy,
shushed and deterred

all would-be passers-by,
your neighbours,
even understanding friends,
emptied them out
like plums from a paper bag
and then folded
and re-creased it
as you have it now?

*

What is there to an empty street
that you will not let it go?
There is no blood,
robbery or impiety
open to the view,
no spectacles required
to see what can be seen,
not even, for certain,
what I've called your melancholy.
So you leave me here,
just as you meant to do,
watching the street.

*

What is there to an empty street?
Is it one of those secret worlds
with metaphysics skulking in the walls,
that door so enigmatic?
Maybe there is something
we might wish to see
face to face, to be
chased from the shadows,

or shaken from the trees
but we never –
These workaday walls are still
the only splendour to be seen.

*

What is there to an empty street?
This time there is a tree,
like a fright wig,
looming above the wall.
The street is embarrassed,
the wall hides itself in shadow,
the corner beetles off
to its secret lodging.
The tree allows two points
of light, like puppets' eyes,
to hold and behold
the bluish scene.

*

What is there to an empty street?
Almost nothing now:
The red wall
the grey wall
the yellow road,
green trees, the blue
of the sky, all simplified,
all still obdurate,
still resisting,
still insisting
they not be named
wall, road, trees, sky.

*

What is there to an empty street?
It seems all that remains.
The corner turns
into the unglimpsed
and none has passed by,
it seems, in ages.
But thus far the walls
and even the trees,
for all their skittering,
appear dependable.
They will not fly off, by Jove,
and leave us darkling.

*

What is there to an empty street?
To be candid now
the terror that it not be there.
Already so much particular
is gone, chased away
by the rage we find
for order: the simply sunlit,
the clearly pure,
the assent to less.
You must have seen it going
before your very eyes,
but you painted on.

*

What is there to an empty street
and yet how easily
I find myself enticed
along your unfathomed carriageway.

And isn't this
what you made it for?
You paint no footfall
but I can hear my steps
and the rustle of my clothes
as I proceed along,
sidling sometimes to pass through
the viewless crowd.

*

What is there to an empty street?
With this one there is the future
possibly, which is always
curving out of sight,
naturally. Out of sight.
But no one wants to see it,
which is why you are alone
and invisible, save for what you see,
what you can't help but see:
the thickening light,
and whoever has gone before
and had to leave you here.

*

What is there to an empty street?
The bruise of the dark corner
as it fades,
the antiquity
of your painstaking lines,
verticals and horizontals,
such composure –
Nice, but how I'd love to drive
a barrel hoop

down your street,
ruddy and exulting,
a boy of nine again.

*

What is there to an empty street?
Well, look hard enough,
tap-tap at it,
wait by the gate,
peer at the tree,
meditate upon the bend,
walk the footpath
back and forth
and patience
will recognise your diligence.
And as the street dissolves
you shall be beckoned.

*

What is there to an empty street?
Do not break your nails
striving to climb the wall,
do not beat upon the gate
and you will flounder
if you try to pass the bend.
Pinch yourself:
this is where you are,
plump and slow.
There is no casement,
enchanted cleft or chasm.
Nowhere to pass or tumble to.

*

What is there to an empty street?
Might it as well be
dead nature,
like a glass of juice,
a cherry and its shadow,
sometimes a cruet?
Dead nature
with its auspices,
even the tree is
motionless and dumb.
Look how stock-still
you will come to be.

*

What is there to an empty street?
But I am drawn to it,
indeed I fall upon it,
it saves me
from looking elsewhere,
saves me from knowledge.
Yes, it will do,
it is as much as I can deal with.
No pundits here,
no hucksters
touting
the difficult future.

*

What is there to an empty street,
as empty as an afternoon,
paused in summer?
Only you are awake
to look at it,

always vigilant,
like the master
standing above his pupil.
Is this it?
Just as you want it?
But that cooking smell,
how long can you bear it?

*

What is there to an empty street?
The relief from indoors,
from what is behind the white gate,
inside the dull windows:
three men in hats
cheating each other at cards;
another solemn *concertino*;
a man on his haunches
with his face in his hands,
others whispering.
It is not free out here,
or genial, only quiet.

*

What is there to an empty street?
Suddenly I notice a lilac tree
spilling over the wall
just in sight, before the bend.
Or it could be plums
so prolific they colour out
the leaves.
How did I not register
so much activity,

the purpling underneath the window,
the purpling sunset
of the waiting storm?

THE NEARLY EMPTY STREET

after Ottone Rosai, via San Leonardo

This is that nearly empty street
breathing in real life.
Should I be surprised
I can find that tree,
the doorway
– both trees–
the lilac and the pine?
How faithful you were,
how devoted to what you saw!
Two funeral cars speed away
disappearing fast,
their office done.

*

This is that nearly empty street:
a parked car
and someone locking it.
A workman's wagon,
drives from your door
plaster-spattered,
step-ladders, trestles,
tubs of paint aboard,
the door left ajar.

This is time, movement,
alteration, your house
not now as you knew it

*

This is that nearly empty street,
changed also
at every moment
by our idling along.
The church porch
stands open to the light and air
of noon, the door-curtain
billowing suddenly.
Here is a secret world
for sure - in those
billows, their restless shapes
promising and concealing.

*

This is that nearly empty street
where sun and earth collude
and the shadows
are for real.
The stone dog thinks
that it commands its own
but look how faint
its image is
cast across the ground,
how frail the tree branch
striving on the wall
but losing itself.

*

For this moment the street is empty,
no *motorino*,
no passer-by,
and we have caught it thus.
The olives on the right
pour shadow
across the paving stones.
The foreground wall
bears all the detail
of abrasion, flake and crack.
Just now, the bend ahead
we can forget.

*

Captured on this nearly empty street
a plastic sack,
packed and tied,
and placed neatly
against the wall
but precious little else
unless, pressing the zoom,
that is a small gate
down to the right
that I might be able,
all unseen,
to slip inside.

*

This is that nearly empty street
teaching me what I can see:
the brass clasps
of some scaffolding;

a circle featured
in the streetlamp's fixings;
one louvred shutter
open at right-angles to the wall;
the stone lion on the gatepost
has graven furrows on his brow,
no bravado –
his moustache almost comic.

*

What there was to your empty street
– I can see it now –
did not rely on shutter speed.
As you painted
your whiskers grew
your stomach rumbled
perhaps your fingers
grew stiffer than they were
and liver spots appeared.
But your street stopped
all that dead.
The paint is motionless.

*

This is that nearly empty street
and we are happy here.
We could do handsprings,
skip rope,
play tick,
anything as long as
we watch for traffic.

This really is *the real world*,
as it is always known:
we got off the bus
just there at the top of the street
and that proves it so.

*

This is the nearly empty street
of the here and now
where parking restrictions
must apply,
messages overfly
and dancing on the spot
becomes obligatory.
Ah this self-excited present,
lulled by its eagerness
not to notice
the tow always underway
out of it.

*

This is that nearly empty street
which can ignore
passages not its own
but still only feign
time cancelled,
or its flow forgotten,
as when we grasp
one moment
of unshadowed joy

and feel the future cannot come,
or at least pretend
its step cannot be heard.

*

Along this nearly empty street
we amble from side to side –
the wet paw-prints
of a curious dog
along a path
could be ours.
There's nothing to speed us,
not the interesting arch
that is
– must I say *is*? –
at the bottom of the street,
or up to now is said to be.

*

This is that nearly empty street.
Does it make you laugh
to watch me treat it
like a metaphor,
that just because
you painted it shut
leaving your meanings
so far inside what seems
without consequence,
I turn up on 'the street itself'
as though my blunt blade
could break the seal?

*

This nearly is 'the street itself',
though what it is
remains still
uncertain yet.
Is it Rosai's mind
painted on out there
or is it the wall
I'm pressed against
as a van comes by?
Is it profitable
to decide on which?
Give me life and give me art.

*

This is that nearly empty street.
However happy-go-lucky
we feel, however
embarrassed the street appears,
it still has our measure.
Its bends beckon us on
not urgently, not insistently,
and only to reveal
nothing much yet,
no smile sinister.
But I look for a bench or a stool
to pause upon.

*

This is that nearly empty street.
Though it looks as it does
it cannot stand still –
there is a car slowing down,

workmen going off for lunch,
whatever moves,
us.
The stone dog and stone lion
show us nothing,
they are all sham,
pretenders, deceivers,
mockers, smirkers.

*

This is that nearly empty street
you had me watching
and which now I am walking on,
cannot help but walk
in the sunshine.
That it is congenial
cannot be denied,
though why might anyone
want to deny such a thing
as sunshine,
a pleasant walk,
life indeed, as it walks.

*

This is that nearly empty street.
I could turn back
but where would
that get me to?
Another street,
but still walking,
gait just the same
though a limp might set in

and I might want to stop.
But even if it takes a litter,
I shall be lifted
and carried forth.

*

This is that nearly empty street
and what is there to it?
Thank you Signore Rosai,
your truly empty street
truly entertained me
and I am grateful for it.
But of course I must walk on,
check the guides again
regarding
that interesting arch,
though I'll still be surprised
to find myself there.

*

This is that nearly empty street
that we have come to see,
nondescript as it is.
We are continuing
our walk,
crossing from side
to side, pausing
conversing,
the three of us together,
merry enough,
and the fourth of us
up in front and now out of sight.

CLOUDS

Here is some time not headlong
but which is just now, quite early morning
when the cloud below us,
but above the lake,
stands in the sun
though just moving, as if herded,
in this case northwards
no commotion.

Nothing is more pacific it seems,
nothing more at ease, not resigned,
at ease,
even as it is carded
and pieced apart
stretched out and combed
as the sun steadily
warms the air.

This going it abides,
no demurral, no recoil
and what that would imply
for time,
until the last wisp possible
is led aside
out of appearance
lost and content.

*

The clouds are to be envied,
did I make that clear?
They are composed,
strangers to anguish,
they accept what comes,
they will not rail
uselessly
rending and howling.

They do not mind
that they will not come again,
the molecules of another day
will belong to that other day
to what this patch
of earth and air
makes up
according to the rule.

Do I make this clear?
Then why, you ought to ask,
should human habit
be so dispraised?
Do we imagine dignity
to give it to a cloud?
Do we imagine questions
to admire what must stay mute?

*

Mute the nature
we always turn to
that has no manners
that does what it does
and fair enough,

so benign the dog-rose
so languid the moon
we are embarrassed.

How have they learned
there is no use in worrying
it never is worthwhile
when it is the while
dawn to dusk, upsets us?
We are the ones who know
the cloud and flower
decease, and it is

their grand indifference,
their immunity to sadness
and to scorn we laud.
Our mind is the stranger here
always ill-at-ease,
always envying
never content to be
the kind of thing it is.

MY CHILDHOOD

In the sound of my pencil
my childhood. It is everywhere
nowadays, like a not unfriendly
scratch, a pin-prick archipelago.

It seems eminently treatable.
Could it even disappear?
A dab of peroxide and cotton-wool

and a little more time again.

But no, it will not depart,
indeed it detains me,
like an arm in a sling,
a leaf blown into a corner.

But that is not truly how it is.
My little childhood plays a merry game
as though still out on our street,
but sees it policy to let me be.

ON THE GRASS

'I do not see us reabsorbed into nature.'

Geoffrey Hill, Odi Barbare *XL V*

I *do* see us this way, or have seen, perhaps see,
no, do see.

See what I have done: I threw my parents' ashes out together
on the grass.

There they would be suffused, blown off, well soaked
and damped in.

And I thought this is not only decent, civil, and
well sanctioned,

but as apt as can be, for this garden, though planted out and
duly mown,

the modern woodland walk titivated and
neatly stepped,

is still kin to those haphazard stars whose hearths will
welcome them.

As we go, here we come, dust-risen, new things
reorganised,

by strange remembrance made and then quickly into
unmaking,

embraced by the wasp's salivered clay, or fire-damp, or
fennel seed.

*

And how restful this promise to bring us home to
nothingness,

to be finished, accomplished, and without
remainder –

I do think I can see this. Yet it is somehow
unsatisfied,

this mind's eye. It was soon looking elsewhere,
its dumb lens

bumping the light, starting to spy itself, trying to
recognise

even one disinterested, helpful thought,
striving to

corner some faith in an unpainted bedroom at
dead of night,

learning how it is of some account,
curious,

unreconciled, keen to get somewhere at least
dignified.

It will die scrabbling. It wants to lift you
from the grass.

BOTH SIDES

these are my parents
whom I know to be dead

yet here they are
at a distance waiting
squashed it seems
into a kiddie-car
gig or dog-cart
– it's hard to tell –
but in a holding pattern
and among the clouds
of course

and they seem composed
even smiling I think
though how can they like
where they are?

what would they want to see?

and on the other side
out of sight among the grass-trees
the as yet unborn
also waiting

TO J. D.

'My dear friend nowhere in sight
This Han River keeps flowing east'

Wang Wēi, 'Mourning Meng Hao-Jan'

1.

My dear friend, where are you now?
Nowhere in sight, not in your half-glasses,
nor turning a page, nor looking askance.

The right bus turns the corner and you get on,
and that's not to be seen again either,
nor your shopper's eye for rabbit-meat or veg.

The sands of Ynyslas, the tides of Forth,
stretch and flow, west and east.
Their inks touch-in the sky but show nothing.

2.

My dear friend, where are you now?
No sight nor sound, no hide nor hair,
nothing but imagined conversation.

A word on Vishnu of the thousand names perhaps –
stuff you knew about – and cool Krishna teaching
that pain is no more to be considered real

than sun, shadow, books, all the familiar clutter.
At the end I think you wanted rid, without
ever being persuaded you were lifted up.

3.

This is your dear and too-European friend asking
where are you now, now you are history,
(as they say)? 'Now' well defined as 'without you'.

As it did become, insistently, for you: '*without…*
without…' until time was no longer history
but held up its hands, unwrote itself,

renouncing pattern, promise, progress, novelty.
What I want now is you here with me
to discuss how that ever could be true.

4.

My dear friend, where are you now? Here I am,
away from your haunts, round the corner
from the sun, hiding from its havoc.

But there are tall, genial flowers here, even hollyhocks,
big sprightly daisies, packed in plots
as you would like, even if every one's an optimist,

and round them a lunkish, tar-black beetle
falls silent for each flower it reaches,
then mithers on. On. Nothing includes you now.

5.

My dear friend, where are you now?
Sometimes I glimpse you in the swagger-land
of dreams – a cut-throat with one fingerless hand

and a plastic sunflower whirring in the wind
trrrrr tick tick tick tick trrrrr...
and some rhubarb steaming.

For all our handsome ingenuity of being
and of mind, such milk-tooth edits
are still the most that's offered us.

6.

My dear friend, where are you now?
I'll be skittish and put you next to Queen
Victoria's Indo-Scottish lover Elphinstone

so you might suss the truth of that old tale;
or, more fittingly, beside your sober-sided forebears,
the missionaries who challenged Vishnu in his lair.

Those are 'the ranks of death' as once understood,
A billet for each deserving novice past the grave.
I would not wish you find yourself alone.

7.

My dear friend, where are you now?
I want to keep this going in imitation
of the industry that's all around:

the birds working the evening draughts,
the flies unfazed by walking upside down,
the mole and worm's unseen and sightless toil,

the snails, avoiding eggshells, seem heedless
and automative. But activity grasps at life
and makes a sort of tribute, not a mockery.

8.

My dear friend, where are you now?
Close enough to sniff, or sense that I am
getting sentimental? No, not that close

of course, but bugs and birds in verses such
as these, offered as companion souls,
would bring out the skeptic scold in you.

Most death has been untimely, miserable –
yours but one – and we want something we can
do about it. Sentiment strives to caulk the wound.

9.

My dear friend, where are you now?
Nowhere, I am sure, where you can see
how I am using you, cribbing you inside

these 9-by-9 lines, yet still faithful to
your taste for rabbit with mustard sauce –
your presence conjured as by a signature dish!

You kept respect, if little *goût*, for poetry,
but even I cannot believe that it can make you
walk and talk, or otherwise give life to thee.

10.

My dear friend, where are you now?
This is the tenth time of asking and enough.
It is a whole number and most complete:

the unit and the zero, what is and what is not.
You broke off and fell that way while
I am still standing, still the upright one,

still numbered, something before nothing
– until the flux resumes
and I will no longer press for where you are.

NOTE

'My dear friend nowhere in sight / This Han River keeps flowing east': from David Hinton's translation of 'Mourning Meng Hao-Jan' by Wang Wēi (701–761) in *Classical Chinese Poetry: An Anthology* (2008).

THE IMMORTALS

JUPITER

O Jupiter, Lord of All as was –
Still just capable of turning over in your sleep
So we ask Grandpa what you said
As if you're still out there when we want to know:
Whom shall we turn to, to whom shall we turn?

But tonight I catch you when I'm caught short
Going home, caught short and whistling,
Gazing up over the rooftops and there you are,
Slightly tangerine, slightly flattened at the poles apparently
And in the telescope moons of your own
To rival the lady herself dropping a veil each night
And briefly you do seem Jupiter, 'stayer of rout',
'Giver of victory', *optimus maximus*, well worth
Your spec on the Capitol since pinched by Marcus Aurelius,
(Equestrian and bedside author, mere mortal).
Dux ductem ductis, boss, boss and boss,
Though where were you when tiny Mr Duffield,
Lost in the Gallic Wars, re-learned each day the savagery of boys?

And where are you now? Long descended from on high,
You're down the hill, elbows on the bar,
Nursing a beer they've named for you;
On good days spruce-ish, bow tie, toothbrush tash,
Button-holing as you detour to the Gents
Where you're gone an age, forehead on the cistern pipe,
Catarrah, yellow, heavy, won't drop from your lips,
Coaxing, squeezing –
You're the sky no longer and cannot show us round.

Just don't do that little dance, Dad –
Landlord will you see him alright?

Let's observe the decencies at least.
Hasn't he got a son somewhere down south?
A Science Park near Rickmansworth?
Some god of background radiation?

VENUS

O Venus, rising from Lurline Bay,
Your one-piece just rolled down,
What is a boy to do but hang on your every word
And especially gesture?
Please come down the beach café.
If you're a photo-shoot I'll post my genes to you,
You're the stock I'd choose alright,
Or if I could give them to you tit-for-tat
How many times would be considered
Extraordinary? O Valeria, Amelia sweet Lianne,
Propitious Queens of Love, we could be at it
Lunch and dinner, feeling the universe move ever outward,
Always to origins not endings, bodies a-tumble,
Not cogitators' mind and soul (how's this for a line!)
O Venus I'm the one to move the earth with you,
Help you with your hawthorn hedges (half-run wild)
Your trodden mires, boot-dung,
Rich and claggy marls, sludge and colt's-foot,
The slopes of rubble that you've colonised,
Your haycocks, bullock pasture,
Jam jars full of spawn,
Your turbid rivers at the flood –
None of this moves but by your love!

*

And if Mars, that real glamour boy,
Skin buffed and glossed, hairless to the drapery-fold,
My best mate, can be drawn to drowse
On your divan leaving his
Lance and tin-hat for the kiddies,
A ribbon cupid-tied around your calves,
I'll not be jealous, I'll not be wronged or peevish,
Nor drunk-distressed, sitting among the ironing,
Steam and starch, cross-legged
Like a little drummer boy, not unreasonable
Though genuinely screwed, fucked over by the mind's
Sexual pawing – *what do you do with him?*
No, I'll not be jealous, for then the fire-step
Could be stood down, the sniper stretch and snooze,
The exhaust in the desert cool
Before the demon finds and enters it.
Soft skin, softly unslain, let him waste
His afternoon with you – hush, by love and reason
It seems that you have done it
And there is no other dream but this.

*

Until, the kiddies learn to dress by the left.
Then boot-blacking the balls of the weakest boy
Will be the least of it. Captain Penus,
When he wakes, sticks it to you once more up the arse
And leaves you to his squad – *by god you should've seen us* –
callow delving, womb-tearing, young boys somehow hating life.

*

And is that you wiping your mouth
Chugging on Listerine ?
Black girl, fucked al fresco on a mattress
in the lay-by dawn till dusk,
International logistics.

*

I have nowhere to go, not my sister's,
And my arms are thin, look, so thin.

Venus, is that you now, can we dare give up on you?
When you totter by and your breathing's bad,
You think you won't go in for coffee,
And don't know what you'd do without TV
And wonder why girls now always show their chests,
We must hang on and hang on
To see one more day of us,
One more increment to our lives
If we can love each other.

APOLLO

Now Apollo, we've not looked at you,
Which of course we can't and thus does your gaze
Make light the perfect metaphor.

Sunny Apollo,
I don't have your eye for stitching, style or shade.
I rose once to wedding-gloves of yellow kid
But I am no handsome *l'homme aux gants.*
You however were only ever once discomfited,
So the story goes, and by your prick of course,

Before reason, and you've long been above all that.
You have no dread of error, no more fear
Of losing an argument than losing a girl.
The white kine sponged down for you,
Trusting heifers lowing upwards to your brow
Are brought to their knees by the spreading springs
Mystified, noses drizzling blood, the finest voices,
Maidens, anointed worshippers.

Indifferent to gory plaudits,
You might turn your head but don't.

Once you were thought time-expired
When out of other blood came the word
That divinity was not a lordling such as you
But some man, skinny, a frowner, shadow-faced,
Eyes black as flies wont to be stapled, pierced,
Twisted by other men and not inscrutable
But ignobly crying out.
Yet as he stood up
and stepped forth, you assumed him without a blink.
His eyes became your eyes of flame,
His wormy pedestal your flawless porphyry,
And below who must be scourged is scourged.
When Regulus, eyelids excised, is turned
Towards you you will not avert your gaze.

The serpent's hymn of adoration says you see everything
And deceive us all – *in the sun dwells intellectual fire,*
What are its eyes?

So are you the One? The one living and True God,
Everlasting, without body, parts, or passions,
Infinite power… wisdom… goodness…

Maker… Preserver… super string… theory of everything?
But we have been learning, Apollo,
We know you what you are.

Because we could not bear the justice of your gaze;
Because you would not blink for anyone;
Because, although you'd slip among us smiling,
Like all the gods you do not really care.
So although we know we will go down with you,
Huddled, glowering, finally chilled out,
How we would love to see you sucked in

And wasted, your light clawed
Back and back, unable to escape,
Dwarfed by degrees, your countenance
The splut of sulphur-springs until
The skull of Apollo enters its own darkness.

Is this peevish? Yes, but you will rise above it,
For it is you who taught us you will die.
Always the modern god, you've made your brain
Downloadable *gratis*,
And show us the idea that through
Many seeings there is one light
And brighter and brighter it will show everything,
Such are our eyes. You will show us everything
And deceive us all. How we sing in adoration,
How we adore the stitching and the shade.

TO HIMSELF

Dreams and systems; humble wishes;
myths that sustain because venerable;
even a walk along the promenade
might do, undertaken regularly.

The sea uprears and then falls back,
turns itself emerald as though auditioning
to be a paradigm, another helpful,
dainty stepper with no power

to explicate or recommend.
So why not fill the time available
as these tall pines have done,
and with no more intent than they?

In fact, dream not, wish not, obviously
believe not. Abandon even the promenade.
As the sea turns itself, strive to imagine
nothing that would stir or stand.

GIVE ME A LINE

Give me a line, any line will do,
it could feature for instance
this periwinkle blue,
it could make a start.

Or I could attend this magpie
on the ledge, he is brisk, fears little,
is at home on brick as much as grass,
he has his place and might be understood.

I like to think that we can make a start
from here, or indeed from anywhere,
you and I, at figuring why we are,
like all else, just so, enabled

to talk and touch, argue and kiss
until we shall be separated,
the world scarcely needing to adjust
as we are so differently disposed.

THE OTHER POEM

Empty windows, empty balconies,
clouds that seem desultory,
only the tree-tops shuffle slightly
in a light wind,
birds go by too fast for the scene.

Nothing else to describe.
Should I lift my head?
Might there be something
to entertain you
over the ledge and in the street below?

The sea is close by –
as it says in the other poem –
but here it is really true.
The sea is a wall it says,
But that I cannot confirm.

I could seek out the gulls
and watch them alight,
taking their nodding
as they walk for greeting,
but that would be fanciful.

The wind from the sea
is now grand and slow –
but that too is from the other poem.
Truthfulness may be all.
I just want a sound I might add in.

SIGNS OF LIFE

on the evergreen continent
a buzz-saw or a sander,
a series of aircraft processing into cloud,
birds intent and attent caw and call,
flowers bloom past convolvulus,

all 'signs of life', making time

trees have grandeur, nothing less,
cicadas stopping and starting in unison,
spiders risking all,
some wrapping-paper blown about the street,
a baker riding pillion home.

SPRING WALK

It is nondescript this long pond,
ignored, left to itself.
The rushes, still straw-yellow
in the early Spring, have maintained
their tenancy, a can and a gin-bottle
disturb them not. They thrive.

Among them, just visible
in ripple and shadow, their cawks
sometimes audible, frogs pursue
their ends: nutriment, spawn,
year into year.

And life can be less than this,
a silverfish on a bathroom tile,
rosettes of lichen plastered on stone,
other mites immobile or invisible.

It seems there is nothing lifeless,
nothing that dares not strive,
nothing that is not open to its death.

IN THE ARMS OF THE TREE

the arms of the cherry-tree certainly beseech,
but what is the point of that?
why plant ourselves inside a common tree?

the people lift their arms to heaven, and perhaps a dove,
their blue sleeves fall back,
they beseech as modelled by what they know

sleeves are the conjuror's stock-in-trade
but the cherry-tree in question
practises neither magic nor sleight of hand

though something here is confusing longing
with the blueness of some clothes
and what might be seen in the posture of a tree.

THE PLAN

A white towel on a washing-hoist
bearing some blurred shadows.

This is but one thing occurring
within the folder of the day,
and of the continent,
and of as far as we can think.

And of course I am watching it now,
liking how the shadows
pause and surge, agitate and swoon,
focus briefly then slide off the edge.

But I am committed also
to common thought
and so am bound to ask how come this,
or anything, is occurring.
What *is* the plan?

The hoist moves left then right,
two steps one way and two the other,
gracefully, like a dancer in the old tyme –
and there comes a likeness barging in,
convinced only likenesses recruit consequence.

Which might do for now and hereabouts
but what is the plan?

THE SWIRL

Am I lost here, as is so often said?
I stand beneath trees I cannot understand,
among rocks that stay closed,
among birds whose styles are quite beyond me.

The painter paints a prospect all his own,
but without trees, only bald arcades and porticoes.
For him at least the swirl is paused.
He knows which way to turn to take his walk.

And that is science! – a way to get by
out in the woods or among the stones,
knowing nothing of them beyond description
but at least which way is up or out.

Words, signals, signs leave naught to go on,
even what was kept from us erased,
until the roofbeam dries to a tinder-crack,
and the lean-to depends less and less,

THE IDEA

Only the sky grey and watery,
little else comes into view,
a tranche of the tree still leafless,
a purple pot upturned,
all bounded by the window-frame.

I am looking for an idea,
something that can connect
these different things –
there are enough of them! –
and will justify me.

But it wants to be left
where it may not be, unspoken,
between this segment of the tree
and the upturned pot,
now less purple than it was before.

THIS WINDOW AGAIN

I'm looking out of this window again.
There is a cabbagy pot-plant
hunkering down for winter, other pots
are empty, rummaged by squirrels.
The trees are starting to bear the marks,
or scars, of autumn and I am up against

meaning once more – is there something
out there on the lawn or am I bound
to make up whatever I will believe
is to be found in a tree or season?

THE WINDOW-LEDGE

Let me not look outside today, but ignoring the lightwell,
the lawn, the tree and all the world outside and what
it might mean, look just at my window-ledge
and its horse-brass screwed into a wooden base;
the tea-bell chased with indistinct Egyptian scenes,
its tinkly clapper long gone probably; a dromedary
kneeling, patient, loaded and ready to rise,
a 'ship of the desert'; and three monkeys
insisting they will see, hear and speak no evil,
all these things the last of the brasses we had at home,
'done' in those days, that is polished, weekly.
Then there is a photo of me perhaps aged 4, smiling nicely
in a white vyella blouse, its plastic frame
no bigger than some foreign postage-stamp
and next to that a tin compass, simple enough
but still able to tell me I am facing south.
More colourful, a china model of Jemima Puddleduck
in her blue bonnet with the avuncular Mr Fox
in his brown waistcoat that Audrey gave me
before she lost her mind - fine work from Beswick's
Beatrix Potter collection of the kind she did herself,
and then two late photographs of my Mum
who in latter days found Audrey a good and cheerful friend.
In one she is raising a glass, not really her

but she *is* at Tom's wedding, in the other she is in her chair
with those two long red candles that were never lit
on the shelf behind. There is another photo of her
with my Dad sitting, I think, near the seaside,
tarpaulined boats in the background,
his arm round her shoulder and both of them
looking so happy. What else? My only
sporting trophy, Longton Schools Cricket Cup 1954
with Florence Primary and my name incised,
and a plaster William Shakespeare seated.
Sundry other photos: the children playing
water-games in Grandad's garden. That in colour,
and Dad in black and white and tie and pullover
looking away from the camera as advised, and
my mother, my wife, my daughter all together.
That old rectangular wind-up clock in green bakelite
always showing half-past eight, morning or night.
Morning or night is what I see beyond the lightwell,
morning then night, morning then night.

IF ALL THIS DID BEGIN

How beautiful our blue-marbled planet from afar,
and so serene, so steady as she goes,
escape-velocity nicely tailored to permit
philately, football and sales of work.

The lizard's silence is not a prayer but is a stratagem.
Likewise warbling of every suit,
a chameleon ambush, the stoat's removal
of her kits, the finery of meadow grass.

The cardsharp of the riverboat saloon
begets descendants, further connoisseurs
of the shortest odds, then a diligent cashier,
perhaps an ever-optimistic therapist.

If all this did begin how might it go on?
And might some understanding, yet to be achieved,
as differently abled as a snake or whale,
recognise a willing purpose and a gracious end?

GREETINGS

1

Good morrow brother louse
(commonest of wood-lice).
Are you content enough
among these paving-stones?
The great star has just
stepped away
and the moon, so self-effacing,
is backing gently
into the light.
Do you need to know this
for your purposes,
and what might they be?
Of course I could research them.
They must include nutriment
for sure, what will keep
your tiny armour
metalled enough,
and your stolid pursuit energised

for as long as necessary –
I note there are fewer of you
abroad today.
But only the sky has control
and might in some form remain
and prove eternal.

2

Good morrow Senhor.
Are you really a lizard
for these parts?
You seem longer than you might
and your kind of green,
virtually viridian,
could draw down
an unwelcome stare.
But here you stand,
motionless
but for the small stomp
of your neck pulse,
sizing up your situation
and what should be
your next serious move.
How much of this attention
are you bound to pay
for safety
and advancement?
This is I'm sure
the same stone universe
wherein we find ourselves.
How like and like
is what it asks of us?

3

My questions are
what they have to be,
as addressed to lice or lizards,
a little pretence
cranking the rhetorical.
I need also speak to clouds
assuming nothing else
will answer,
as though believing
they will tell me true
how we are
under this local sun,
crouched at a table
or stretched on a low divan
and under instruction
from every galaxy
alive and dead.
Thank heavens
that these pink flowers
balanced
on their slender stems,
these plums,
gripping the tree,
can almost be described.

4

… 'can almost be described',
by mugging up on pistils,
or through such words
as might be beautiful,
though with nothing of the flower?

But neither will forestall
the remorseless re-wind
into questions.
And how proud is this mind
to see these things invisible,
the knowing coils
it can find to grapple with,
heaving itself
above the unworthy ruck –
'Look I am good at this,
I really am!
And I exist!'
That lizard I have not seen again,
the wood-lice are past their season,
clouds come and go –
so why should I care for them,
they are no more than presences.
What I can entertain is here,
far beyond the nameless stars.

5

Unless – is this a threat
or a promise? – *unless*
we already know what is
the only real abstraction.
This mind will go
its long way round,
fancying the eternal
lies in perfect circles
and the no-name god,
devising every kind of dazzle
to believe it can confuse
death's set coincidence

and scratch itself
a toe-hold in eternity,
but only side-steps
what hides before us.
Death is what it is, stupid,
nothing more
philosophical than that.
We are as palpable
as the lizard, louse
and cloud with whom –
must I say? – we can
almost be described.

THE LAKE

The red slipper of the dawn steals across
the line of hills, its confidence today
just as before. Hard to understand how
it might seem tentative as it captures
and lights the waiting lake. The whole day
then stirs, shrugs and follows suit.

*

The lake stands there between the trees,
even behind the trees, out of sight, but
still there – of course it is, whether grey or
blue, it stands there to reason. Does something
stipulate that there is knowledge of this
kind, something inscrutable yet plain?

*

The weather breathes upon the lake.
Suddenly everything is beautiful
especially that distant inlet
and the white boat with its fisherman.
He proceeds inwards, beyond my sight,
his landfall surely embraced by trees.

*

It is to one side and well below where
my mind sits and stares at the darker patch
on the farther shore which was yet darker
and a different green. But now that patch
is lost. A cloud-shadow is all it was, though
it seemed so anchored in the noble scene.

*

I was looking for a face or sign upon
the waters' flat impassive span
but there's nothing – an unconscious
cloud-shadow, nothing notable, only
obedient part-work, sad creature
of the casual battlements above.

*

Imagined as bodies for the umpteenth time,
these shadows on the wood
seem 'dragonish', imperious,
exhaling themselves proudly across
the humble trees before vanishing
piecemeal, nonchalant, unconcerned.

*

The significance of the lake falls away
so strive to hasten it as it goes,
tear from its false countenance
the last vestment and last humour
fetched from afar to colour in
its brazen vacancy.

*

Ah these 'many states of the soul'
hard by the margins of the lake.
Gaura and willow-herb might be confused
by an unpractised eye. Neither
belongs here. Nor these deadheaded roses
flickering into further bloom.

*

Now here comes the thunder and whatever
it is saying nowadays, barrels
rolling downstairs towards us in the vaults
or caverns of a children's story.
The lake absorbs it all, lightning included,
and needs not even brace itself for harm.

*

A dead tree still standing high above
the lake is a solemn, and a sorry sight.
But it is the martins' misericord, where they rest
from their frantic labours, climbing and diving
in the speck-laden air, their lake of fishes,
their high veldt of game, their ocean shoals.

*

Across the other side six poplars
stand sentinel by the shore.
Upright, military, their being is surely
all martial, just as their opaque cousin
cypress holds death
deep inside its dense and wary heart.

*

In full sun, at midday, the lake is not
at its best, its colour is uniform,
leaden, every kink in the shore
readily there and nothing given
to mystery, beholden to no incident
nor sensing anything incipient.

*

Shrink-wrapped hay-bales glint above the shore,
their shine part of the sun's work at this hour,
as are stray windscreens and sun-roofs
whose owners are shaded somewhere, botanising
perhaps, or tidying their samples
and paperwork for calls this afternoon.

*

There is no signal on the surface here
though currents must ride through open doors below.
Some conditions will bring driftwood
into view, each piece finding other debris
to form slow rafts that seem piloted
towards the patient shore.

*

Of point and purpose: how intelligible
is the lake? Its irrigations are the reason
for the village drowned but what of
its colours and misshapen mists,
need these be understood?
How daring must the mind be now?

*

I've not heard, nor heard of, any church-bell
beneath the water, nor of anyone old
tied to a chair as the waters rose.
Perhaps there was a cat stuck up a tree
out of earshot. All else decamped to higher ground
leaving so much to a different world.

*

No flesh-footed shearwater fetches up here –
wrong salination, wrong trade-winds,
wrong hemisphere divided east and west.
Even so-called local gulls pass this lake
which means that, being unfrequented,
I can make it lonely and so sorrowful.

*

Ocean waves must beat upon the shore,
they cannot turn aside. They are raging
to be free but hopelessly. The drowsy lap
lap at the shelving of the lake never seems
agitated or ill-at-ease but is content
to live as it lives. It has found its bond.

*

Still. Stillness. Why do we, who must move
to live, hanker so much for tranquillity?
Why do we want the lake to be 'like glass',
for there to be 'no breath of air'?
Stillness is the chamberlain sent on ahead –
we should racket and bang our pots and pans.

*

Some tiny figures, seemingly in black
from here, patrol the farther shore.
What might be washed up for them?
A single plimsoll will be no use
and only the rarest bottle or ancient shard.
The lake's gift is their expectation.

*

An aircraft that can't be seen grinds
its way above the lake, finding,
before it passes on, some regard
of what it sees below, the lake's whole shape,
its interesting, haphazard outline
that I so long to see entire.

*

I want to find some pattern in the lake,
something in twelves since that is what
I was given early to fit around the world –
the shilling, the Apostles, inches to the foot.
But it will not do, nor any crystal shape.
Nothing straight-edged can resolve the scene.

*

I watch the lake between the trees,
its sheen goes silvery in the evening light.
How much it changes and so challenges
these quite capable and hard-working words
leaving them wan and out of sorts.
Not so much has been achieved.

*

Dusk. Along the skyline a lemon-yellow
sunset turning orange. A solitary light,
high in the trees, comes on, the first to ward off
the fearsome dark. Then others follow,
clutching at their own relief
until only the lake is blackness.

BELVEDERE

Even up here we cannot think we see it all.
Trees, grass, haze, vines, a bird
hastening horizontally across,
and so many creatures and human things holed up:
a badger that will be abroad tonight,
a stone fountain dried out and overgrown.

I could begin again with other instances:

the nearly-yellow track angled against the wood,
a snail clutching the iron footing of a post,
unrippled water on the lake,
a stationary boat in silhouette,
closer by, some friendly human murmuring.

Yet we keep the will to understand it all.
We watch the wireworm and the humming-moth
as best we can; study the undersoil;
figure river-tides and how they might be tamed;
invent gradations to suit the way we see,
but still are pestered by so much profusion.

So what we do is make this stand for this,
as representative, pretending there is enough of
every single tree to make it one with
every other single tree despite a shivered branch,
or whatever stance it offers to
the awkward sky. We must do this

or be swept away – fixing that single name inside
our careful and uncoloured mind
as the clearest beauty we can know.
But life is there only in every separate thing,
each flutter of a dream near the edge of sleep.
We would not wish less of ourselves to be recognised.

DREAMS OF LENNOX ROAD

Lennox Road is always in my dreams.
Lila, winning a race, scudding over the grit
and puddles, is always on Lennox Road
though she has never been there, knows nothing of it.
It is my dream alone, though surprisingly hospitable.
It holds me, clasps me to itself
as though, independent as it seems, it has need of me.
Lennox Road, the place and name, always in my dreams.

#

'You're walking well today,' I say, drawing level.
It's uphill, but not too steep, it's Chaplin Road.
He smiles but does not speak. I take his arm.
Perhaps it is his shoes, white plimsolls
and three pairs of socks, the last one white
and turned over. His duffel coat is from 1965,
black and only done up half-way.
We stop where I turn off for Lennox Road.
He must carry on up, on his researches.
It is Lilian Gish that he must find he says.

#

How can you belong here? The dream says we are
in Lennox Road but you and it are not quite right,
though the margin out the back, some grass, garages,
fruit-canes and an entryway could be that particular ground.
Were you waiting there for me to come near the back-door,

perhaps to put something out, so that I would see you
overflowing that child's chair in a voluminous
and confusing dress? You were nearly an enemy
but you're smiling now, though I'm still uncertain
and don't know whether to approach or speak.
And who are you beckoning to as though off-stage,
and are you saying 'Look, here he is'?

#

I'll need a taxi home from here.
I ask him 'Take me to Ch… Ch… Chaplin Road.'
There it is in my mind's eye with a map
but I know that's not where I go now, going home.
But nothing else, no other name will appear…
Ch… Ch… Ch… Chaplin Road… until
slowly it clears and is replaced by now.

#

Clothes all over the floor, shirts, ties, trousers, underwear,
as though drawers have never been filled.
It feels like it must be the wrong dream,
an image perhaps from some book I've read,
but no, it insists, this is Lennox Road indoors,
but with nothing familiar, no view, no window,
but still it insists, this is Lennox Road.

#

Yes, this is Lennox Road again,
from the back garden this time,
and from the rockery end,
his back to the house, an Australian
is bowling and I am quite confident.
But the ball takes my hip or bat-handle
and I am caught for naught.
Back up the rockery steps I go
and one who is sitting chewing
says nothing as I go past.
They are wearing maroon caps
but this is an Ashes Test!

#

We are the chosen venue!
For the closing event, the final jamboree!
Crowds of everyone are here
and along Deggs' path next door
children from schools process
with flowers in their hair and holding hands.
The dignitaries are taking their place
above the garden, all looking slightly Edwardian
a few wing-collars, somewhere a silver band.
I am the MC, standing up on our back step
but such is the acclaim no word is required.
Geoffrey steps forward – it is like the opening
of a public park or railway – he starts to read.
A tear shows in his eye.

#

no dreams of Lennox Road for months now

in this other world my father was first to leave
exasperated and beginning to panic that afternoon
(a nurse noted that shaking her head)
and he was gone that very same night

then my mother, *piano piano* through weeks
of who knows what kind of sleep
or wakefulness, until one afternoon, out of the sun
she slid away, leaving her body
which carried on changing anyway

so there are all my indwellers of Lennox Road
departed, pencil-shavings caught in the air,

though they might or might not re-appear
in the random play of dreams

my brain bringing them along, an occasional reflex,
perhaps a gift, but in some guise
not of their choosing nor of mine

#

this is Lennox Road, that I know,
though it is the other end
where we are playing on the bricks
and the device we have is not working

it is a box but the numbers

on each of its screens flicker
and turn themselves back to front,
it is broken, finished, irreparable,
we cannot play though this time
I don't know who we are

then – just like that – one says
'I'll go and get another'
and yes, there at the end of the street
is Pye's sweet and lolly shop,
Mrs Pye with her big refrigerator,
and here in this dream she had one in
and someone brings it back with only
this afterthought of coins
and we settle on the kerb again

#

again at the other end
amid the old houses
I have an address but I'm not sure
and I knock on a door
no answer
but next door responds
and it is Dorothy whom I seek,
she does not look like her
but it is, I can see

just then the other door
opens a space,
an old lady there though she stays

behind the door, not speaking,
I try to explain
she stays in the dark of her house
I look to Dorothy
and am at a loss

#

I'm at the other end, the old houses
and the poorer end
and my friend (whom I do not recognise)
goes to her friend's to ask for me
if she knows

she comes to the door, friendly,
and asks us in over the broken step
(I wonder where is the man who should fix this?)
there is a child too
and the house is all for her
on every wall
on every surface
and hanging from the ceiling
are toys and decorations
soft toy chimps, teddies and dolls,
plastic games, bagatelles,
an irrepressible jack-in-a-box
that seems alive and must be
stuffed into a wall repeatedly

#

I wake in my old room
though I know I am grown-up now
and I just know I am alone here

I lurch out of bed
and with but one mis-step
get to the door
and to the bathroom
where the bath is as I remember it
but the toilet bowl not
until the room is filled in
as by a sketch-pencil working fast
an invisible help

#

We have finished our training
and somebody and I hit the New York streets
as drummers, door-to-door salesmen
of TV Sport packages.

George is first to answer the door,
he has glasses and smiles warmly.
'But what I would like,' he says,
is a package for theatre and the arts.'
'That can be arranged,' I say.
'I live close by, I can bring you
the brochure information that you need.'
'Thank you,' says George, 'I'll wait for it.'

And I go back to the street
which is Lennox Road for sure.

#

This is strange. It's been a fast trip home,
five hours by car, but from Australia.
We draw up outside No. 10,
parking under the gaslamp.
A woman in a straw hat, not our sort, with a child
is walking down our path
passing through the garden it seems,
used to it since we have been away.
Then we – who are 'we'? –
are indoors but next door, in Deggs' house, No. 12,
looking out of their window.
And where are they?

#

Pedalling 'furiously'
I turn the corner into Chaplin Road,
slightly uphill,
and it is suddenly slow going,
the brake-blocks
are sticking on the rims
more and more
till I drag to a stop
foundering.
Lennox Road is still up there ahead.
I won't make it back there now.

#

This one is different.
I have flown home to check everything is ok.
I am at the back door of Lennox Road
at first hard shut.
Then I can open it into that scullery
and our old dog that never lived there.
Everything is in order into the living room.
All as it should be.

#

We stop to take a photograph
but as we do a yellow taxi
corners at speed, almost on two wheels
with the rest of our gang hanging out the windows
laughing and cheering
on the way to the war.
And yes, it is Bengry's shop
on the corner, the corner of Lennox Road.

DRAWING LESSONS

after John Ruskin

'Now if you can draw that stone, you can draw anything'
The Elements of Drawing

for Brian Maidment

*

look your stone antagonist boldly in the face

I do. I mean, *I try*. I falter but do not fall back.
I will valiant be! It is not my pencil,
nor my hand but the bounds of my attention
that have no membraned stuff tough enough.

How does a stone wait for us? At the ready?
Why does it antagonise so? Resistant
to all entreaty, obduring, yet what might
it relieve us of? What could it pillage?

Then why must I stand up, why try to seize
and satchel the likeness of a stone?
Is this how to live on the earth about us,
believing a stone is honoured by a line?

A stone, a leaf, their fragile shadows clinging –
we are not of them however proximate they seem.
And yet 'their fragile shadows clinging'
will adhere. How do I muster a tender act?

the best drawing-masters are the woods and hills

You are my best drawing-masters, you and your kin
and I am instructed. But does my pencilling
bring me towards a sight of you,
even to a glimpsing, the moon inside a cloud?

Everything is human, nothing looks itself:
the leaf is sorrow bent, the willows
cradle-arch the headlong stream,
the waters either errant or stymied in their pools,

the trees clustered but still   unneighbourly,
even you, old stone, junk from a hapless cliff,
are harried and beset,
made but to serve my cognizance.

O tree, stone, air, babbling brook, will you not be yourself!
I see you sometimes strolling sometimes spry,
but only ever as you are not, captured
again and again just so, but nothing like.

dense and unmalleable this world

Dense and unmalleable this world indeed,
so what is to be done? Stories try to
hoick it into order, patting it like butter
or a brick, something to put a finger on,

a dish or a flight of consequences.
But how do they end? vain loves and fruitless deaths.
The pencil line at least is modest, no exhilaration,
often a wholly grey or rainy day is best.

In such a light tree-boughs stand like dark rivers
against the sky, the sky like long-fallen snow,
and I'm trying again at my spiny conker-shells:
can I get them to split upon the page?

Oh my scuffed, rubbed, dirtied patient page,
there seems nothing between the world and you
but in some shape it stays out there.
Is there a tender point, a tender thought to move it?

mew and howl

mew and howl how much indeed do I mew and howl,
not for the drudgery of shading but for the whole
codge-modge I am making –
the lines off-beam, the shadowing

too profound, the volumes pancake-flat,
and as I rub and rub and try again
the stale bread I use scratches and maims
this smudged, fingerprinted and dishonest page

and crumbles about the room. Yet I must go slow!
I know that the swish of a line drawn
with what is called freedom is wrong,
as leaving bread to waste upon a window-sill

is wrong, that I should never let my natural hand
think it might go free, that hereabouts is nothing
but itself. Better the codge-modge, I'm thinking.
I cannot be God, not even on a page.

Nature will show you nothing if you set yourself up for her master

And why not, pal? How much poke does she think she has?
Look at these naïve potato-flowers,
so silly, so virginal, they are bound to look my way,
the orange-tree, for all its spikes, cannot act

rebarbative enough. Turves, a slouching hare,
another sunless copse, fields without folk,
the charcoal tumble of a mountain stream,
a makeshift grotto in the rocks above,

my cross-hatched lilies, all these stand there,
dutiful and still, not an itch not a twitch.
For Nature has nothing new to show,
nothing unanticipated, unforeseen,

unmined and unrefined, nothing my stylus
cannot incise, nothing unbidden by guile
or charm or force. I am set up,
a master and bestride; Nature moonstruck, daft.

shutting the light gradually up (i)

The faintest of lines drawn across the page
sets this process off; a bucket of pitch,
a broad brush, heavy-laden, becomes logical,
and we see the end of art is blackness.

So what now? Thankfully, some strides are easy,
especially in thought, and just one
will take us to the Half-Way House
licensed for the sale and consumption

of alcoholic beverages in some full name
always neatly legible beneath the transom
of etched or frosted glass. Inside, the varnished
wood is styled in brushed horizontal strokes

and everywhere there are circles to be seen,
coins, beermats, stools, fixings of many sorts
and hues and patterns in clothes, labels, skin.
Though never untouched, light does pass.

shutting the light gradually up (ii)

Meanwhile, back at the artists' camp, the light had changed.
Was this a 'trick', a variation of the variation
slyly declined from its routine pilgrimage?
Light holds so many options it can ignore habit,

and even though we artists exult in this
we cannot keep up – now we see it now we
see it otherwise. Loosed from the sun
light turns us without mercy or regard,

so many particulars, special cases, glimpses left aside:
that's a dry leaf scurrying not a snake or a shrew,
a tree cut off against a now truncated sky,
a weir-stone turning its water into perfect glass.

Weary of this we are, just like the mythic soul
who journeyed on in timeless and perpetual light
until she sat, closed her eyes, and shutting the light
gradually up, gave us the darkness and the night she dreamed.

there's a line and a natural line

there's a line and a natural line
but what you will ask of course is how
anyone can be that definite. The line defines
is all I can say, which is convenient.

In latitudes where the sky is lineless
you can wait all day to limn a cloud-edge.
Swing-ropes tautened by a broken seat
hang there as stand-ins, their twinings and plaitings

made natural by gravity you could say,
a convenience that I imagine as
stair-rods, cartoon rain, lines heading straight down
something as natural as you can get.

But the bough curves upwards and the hand
strives to follow it, leaps to think that it has found
the natural line and cries out boldly:
'Look, we are as one! Me and this patient tree!'

there was a spacious half of seat vacant in my little hooded carriage

Verticals, horizontals, diagonals, antagonists all.
A line that ought to be approaching neatly
saunters suddenly aside, takes the perspective
so the void collapses and the space is lost.

The paper neither smiles nor scowls, an ice-dive
could find no mischief there however deep it is.
I could arraign the always-otherness
of natural things like the four pines across

the near-horizon, five when I look again.
Yet all the world out there demands is some attention.
Four or five? That at least. They even stand
stock still this morning as though to be of help.

Snow falls on the river and is then something else.
On some scaffolding that man in a high-vis tee
must watch his step. Better his foot does not find
a gangplank changing into vacant air.

...creatures who are every instant perishing ...

... creatures who are every instant perishing ...
like a waterfall: there and at the same time vanishing;
always ellipsed but always with us.
They leave me tongue-tied but never leave.

Because what is instantly helpful to creatures
who are every instant perishing is ...
revolving this is a regular shame.
Let me be helpful, in pencilling and elsewhere.

I draw a bar tightly across a page
and set to work. To one side
I scribble and scribble to a coalhouse black
and then seek to shade stealthily

toward the other side, greyer and lighter
with every touch into the page's patient white.
Dissatisfaction with what I do is wholesome, but I might
graduate to show some creature in the twilit sky.

the best answerer of questions is perseverance

The beauty of the light needs not to be
attested to, it boils and shudders anyway,
so to see things in themselves is to possess
composition enough – that can be securely said.

But then the gusts of sunlight unman me,
even as I lift my eyes to meet it
line and mass dissolve again just as I
duck beneath the parapet.

To be so lost in it, feeling blind,
no more than scrabbling as though this world
were lightless and once more the pencil blunts,
breaks and even the page begins to snigger.

The best answerer of questions is perseverance,
That will not be of the saintly kind
but that through wind and weather, all I am allowed
to help me seek whatever waits inside the light.

it would be bad advice that made you bold

But what scares me is to be thought
pusillanimous – 'Da da dee da da!
What yer waiting for Wainy?'
and meanwhile here comes Big Ballsy

pounding down the slope, going hard for it,
the big doffer, up and over the brook and –
nearly makes it, he falls back on landing,
you can see he's wet through to his pants.

But he dunna care, he beats his chest, he's ready
for the Cabaret Voltaire and grabs a megaphone:
DOFFERCOCKSTERBROCKSTERDOO –
surely this is 'the language of Paradise'!

But Ballsy had gone about as fer as he could go
and took up his pen again. 'I never could bid
chaos welcome' he wrote, and I am daunted anew.
Labour on therefore courageously.

You will never love art well till you love what she mirrors better

… what she mirrors better. Is shadowing then
what she is about, and why we are so enamoured,
so very smit by colour and by sock-wool
figured from a herring's useful skeleton?

Perhaps, but this makes me drawn to devilry.
R's modest 'what' is of course venerable
Ma Nature, our mother even when she was only
glops, molt and flame, not the jovial dame

of ladysmock, author of zephyrs and the noble nod
of cedar, oak and lime, who preceded
and must take precedence, making us feel small
as even pismires are revealed as better organised.

This is not how I choose to be chastised.
When I seek the shadow what looks back is human,
as mutable as a leaf or the artist's eye,
which looks and then makes up what it sees.

WHAT AM I SEEING?

'What sort of human, pre-eminently human feeling it is that loves a stone for a stone's sake, a cloud for a cloud's.' – Ruskin

(1)

Why are there trees and bushes in the snow?
I could ask a weathergirl – she knows which way the wind blows.
Whichever - they are easy to get at and easy to pass by.

Another kind of question is
why has the brush painted
'Trees and Bushes in the Snow'?
Or 'A Bowl of Fruit', especially without
its tell-tale, vacated sea-shell lying conveniently by?
Why go to all that trouble of painting it
when you can have the real thing easy as pie?
(Sometimes I like to call a pie a pie, or a pie.)

But it *is* possible to worry here.
Granted, 'A Bowl of Fruit' is not a bowl of fruit,
for it can be – especially if a touch discomposed –
colour freed from line, or lines strolling, or 'structure',
and thus even a piece of the true universe;
and it may not have to work hard
to take me out of myself in the same way as an arena
of shadow under a kitchen-chair
is a version of the snow-capped roof-tiles opposite,
or, as another house does when it casts a witch-shadow,
again in the snow, so that I ask myself
'What *am* I seeing? What is *also* there? What is *really* there?'
and 'is this a good question or should I fetch the apples and the pears?'

(11)

After Guercino. 'The Assassination of Amnon'

Amnon cops it at table, plates, apples and pears tumbling.
A left-cross topples him,
exposing his neck and throat, a brown patch of shadow
pointing in a 'v' towards the breast-bone,
shading off upwards towards the temple
so that the cheek can be just paper
turned from the dagger that is already coming down
in the fist of the second guest, inked in dark
beneath the handle, and then the blade bare to light
as it reaches the scribbles of his hair
and the two days' growth pen-scratched beneath his chin.

I too want to see the world as an arrangement:
the tunic bucklings and seams as interruptions
of light and that light washed gently over
so that the armpit appears, then the dark head and beard,
the tip of the second dagger also heavily inked in
until out of the empty white come the two guests.

*

Except, upon further investigation, they are not guests
but servants, seconded from the work of beasts
to the work of men. Here is the justice of it.

Amnon cops it, but what looks like treachery is,
we will understand, true recompense.
Amnon has raped his half-sister, the girl-child *Tamar*,
though, as she says, had he asked the king for her
the king would not have demurred,
but *Amnon* raped her and then hated her

and had his servant bolt the door against her.
Rent, weeping, ashes upon her head,
she goes to her brother *Absalom*, himself half-brother
to *Amnon*, who guesses right and says:
'Hold now thy peace sister: he *is* thy brother;
regard not the thing.'
And she goes in and the story leaves her,
And we do not know if this brawl of justice
ever comforts her, or why, truly,
Absalom sees to it that she is avenged;
or if it is justice the brush and pen wants to show
or movement in ink.
'Get the line and shade more tender':
As you see a stone so you see a man.

WHO WAS ST CHAD?

In memory of my mother

Did God speak to Nell the way
that Anselm heard Him clear?
From Sandford Hill it was hard
to imagine the court of Christ,
the air not rare enough
to let her through.

O Longton in your photographs,
marvelling at your famous ovens,
the bottles of smoke, the soot, the dirt,
the blackened bricks, the sun
lost to the long flame
and its buried fire.

Here Nell listened for the obscure
voice of God, assuming nothing.
She knew she must abide
this darkness, the salt-cloud
of unknowing rolling up
Anchor Road towards the fields above.

It's my guess God stayed mum,
no rapturous bang or wallop,
nothing seraphic, nothing
stigmatical like that visited
on gaunt, vision-ready girls
in mossy grottos far away.

Did she worry much that He stays
unseen, this nevertheless living God,
this puzzle-setter *than whom nothing*
greater can be thought… who is
whatever it is better to be
than not to be etcetera?

She did not nourish doubt –
how could she spare the time? –
though when her sister
mocked her for her churchy ways
she longed for a sign
that would shut her up for good.

Sid, her other half, liked
to argue the toss
that folk who went to church

were the better for it,
better occupied than Mrs H
off to their 'van every weekend.

Taking a bag of toffee-rolls
to Ray, now too breathless
to say 'thanks', that's a Sunday job,
not fixing up a deckchair
and then four pints in the *Sailors' Rest*.
Never went to church himself though.

Smoke, travail, the scratch edges
of biscuit-ware, the saggar-men
heavy-laden. Rising early
on Sundays grants an hour
separate from the rest
and with all those different words.

1908 a brickwork boom:
St Chad came out of the rain
at Adderley Green,
Hugh Bourne lustily
memorialised along Stone Road,
his hefty chapel brimful of folk.

The sidesman would say, though only
to himself, 'I'm an ordinary man,
just a man in socks,
but when I'm in here it's different,
I don't feel so described.
We should all feel that way.

'And there's good things on this earth:
bringing you clean and
well-wrapped up from the
Cottage Hospital. Hard then
to think of sin and all that.
The serpent has to sleep betimes.'

'Why is there summat and not nowt?
Tha dustna know, but think
a' this. If we wasna here,
all on us, milling rind,
He'd have no reason to exist.
It's Him depends on us.'

And they dug in and sang, all around
their work-space dirty with white dust,
chapel and church at odds
but both defiant against
time and motion. To the worthy world:
this is the Lord's day, not yours.

St Chad's always smelt too high
for most local tastes
but it was the scent of her girlhood,
a small touch of beauty,
a six-candle gleam,
all Father Cooper's parti-coloured copes.

Father Cooper, a mission priest,
though the 'heathenish estates'
came later, was the loveliest man.
He gave her a Shakespeare,
Warne's Chandos Classics much-prized,
not much read. Was he the form of God?

Or at least the form of Man,
with a smile for you, not like men
must be on Sandford Hill, not like
her father, his innocent tobacco-knife,
his vengeful strap. The priest
could listen, even to a girl.

It's him she remembers deep in
the Ordinary Time,
the yearly plod to Advent.
Through every dull Epistle
she remembers him and Chad's
silvery morns, the one bright spot.

Nell was a modest lady all her days
who always took her turn
to do the flowers,
iron the vicar's surplice,
vacuum all around. 'Drudgery divine'
she's heard it called, more than once.

She let herself in with the cleaner's key.
Closed inside that mysterious
diapered brick she liked the quiet.
The professors say the universe is silent
but with stars colliding there must be
something to be heard. She listened.

Wherefore did we make a noise?
The band of the Boys' Brigade –
her brother Perce was a bugler in that,
he was chapel – drumming street
by street in springtime, the big lad
making his gladsome noise unto the Lord.

Or just enjoying himself.
Gladsome is how we should live,
even under judgement,
glad to know we can survive
without sting, without sighting
the orange fire unquenchable.

Gladsome we should be
even if we believe none of it,
should not be brazen
but gladsome in living as though –
as though there will be some
reckoning, some sort of quittance.

Some rapatag broke into church last night,
trashed it looking for cash
and left a steaming dump.
She cleaned it up of course
saying to herself
'Who knows where's sacred nowadays?'

The old tin chapel rusted to death.
The Prims' tabernacle, bathroom supplies.
Chad's hosts Weightwatchers on Wednesdays.
Who needed the Tuscan demi-columns
of St John's? Dresden Methodist
New Connexion 'since demolished'.

'By the end there were only four of us
regular. Harry and Philip had died
the same February and Ada said
she'll not come again unless
her son could drop her off – he'd not come
himself – why don't they these young folks?'

With the mighty Bourne now gone for
starter homes, its folk all in their heavens
somewhere beyond the Crem,
none of us these days worries much
where we are bound but click
and collect a longer life.

The preacher was right to rail
at rock 'n' roll. Bill Haley's
careful kiss-curl beckoned us
up stairways we'd never
dream dream dreamt about
and we just got shaken loose.

This is our modern life: first an inside lav.,
a motor-bike and sidecar,
then a smart saloon,
vaccinations against so much,
Reason lightens every load.
We don't need no story anymore.

Then it's all so frantic nowadays.
The big shop on Sundays,
get to the sales for school shoes,
sometimes a trip to Legoland.
These are not Vanities, we are not
living deliciously or waxing rich.

We do not love our kids the less.
We may be seen to check our phone
while grandma struggles for a word –
not in itself a mortal sin.
I'm sure any of us would cross over
to help a body fallen in the street.

But God we do not seek, early or late,
we thirsteth not nor longeth now it seems;
life's here and must be lived
somehow, making the best,
counsellors are often wonderful
and there are joys to be had.

Though how can we be the first
to live without the need
for pleas or prayers,
without imagining
a face in kindly stone – ,
or s*ummat* listening and taking heed?

By our vases do we mourn:
Dearest Grandad – Gone Fishing …
reunited… locked in our thoughts.
Kleenex balled in every hand
we grieve to find the words
to measure up to measured death.

We want to know what's true here.
Is it all done with?
Was Perce but matter, a sister's love
never necessary, aimless,
tending to no end?
We need to know these things.

Nell had all the grand antitheses:
Though he were dead yet shall he live
though… worms destroy… yet in my flesh;
though and *yet* looked hard
and made their offering untrembling.
The thing, Death, nailed by common words.

Though she mourned yet was she comforted
though she was comforted yet did she mourn.
In words her God was nearly visible
perhaps there and everywhere.
She probed for Him most near Perce:
Was Christ there as he died she knew not how?

Was Perce, via the Boys' Brigade,
so comforted? Knowing that,
she would have been so comforted
that Christ was by as someone sought
proper burial words to help
his soul past a false oblivion.

Or does Christ stop sometimes
by Longton Cenotaph on Trentham Road,
a ghost in his Light of the World garb
but still mortally unseen,
and invigilate awhile, though Perce
is absent from the roll? God knows why.

Though she mourned yet was she comforted,
though she was comforted yet did she mourn
in her bedsit, behind her night-curtain.
Did she feel blessed, and so not alone?
What did those words do?
Who was St Chad, known to welcome rain?

What comes up when you google Death?
Not much. Sites don't like to commit
beyond 'permanent cessation' and
'mystery'. There are quotes on 'Good Reads'.
Was it better to hearken to it weekly:
dust and ashes have no dominion?

I always wonder why I visit
ashes. Clearly it makes no difference
to these long-gone bits of calx
as I stand here dutifully
once a year, an unbeliever.
They are gone but will not absent themselves.

They will persist, pursue us
'down the years'. Or is it we
who mither them, striving
to drag them back to artificial light?
All that matters most is invisible.
Now we think that, now we don't.

Death as it appears to us
will not be solved, nor yet finessed.
Chad tried, Anselm tried, Nell tried
and though there is so much about us
that was once unseen, Perce and the angels
will not vouchsafe themselves.

Bodies chucked down slopes, bodies
never found, bodies reverently washed,
all dead, finished with.
And if the soul is there it slips
away, though still spoken of
as the word at the core of us.

Or else a piece of the body's
brainwork made (up)
to dignify its faecal dross,
a compliment we can't resist –
'we' not knowing what we are
any better than we know St Chad.

MY FATHER AND 'THE ONWARD TENDENCY'

Because he could not bid chaos welcome
he railed at me who made a botch of long-division.
Yet how could he not respect Arithmetic
when it had saved him from the pit,
from long days a mile under North Staffordshire,
familiar injuries, coal-veins from every cut and scratch?
Instead clean hands and nails, a trilby
and a decent gaberdine, his foolscap ledgers
without a blot or smudge safe every night.
It was not much, but better,
and if I could master long-division
and the rest I might be a Dr Salk or another of the heroes
by whose deeds children are plucked
from iron lungs and fearsome calipers,
saved by sun-lamps and the proton beam.

So he thought we were on our way, not blithely
cresting the wave in gangshow singalongs
nor on the town with GI Joe and dames,
but modestly, always tipping his hat,
finding my second-hand bike, the best tinned fruit
we could afford, evap. or long-life cream,
my Sunday trousers always tailor-made.

I guess he was happiest in 1951:
the Nazis done and dusted, had paid their frigid tribute
in a tent at Lüneberg and Britain was *in festa.*
It was all contemporary: he was on the train
with just my Mum to see the Skylon
floating 50 feet above the ground,
the future he had always looked towards,
its rubric newly set in *sans-serif,*
everything discovered under just one dome,
dress-prints designed from crystallography!
Yet within the year modernity was scrappage,
down the river on Churchill's vengeful barge.

How much of the future can you expect?
Counting up he must have known Royal Art
was down the pan, that Mr. Aubrey,
trying to park what once was Peter Sellers'
Cadillac in Commerce Street, could not add up,
subtract, divide or multiply, found pots and plates

too heavy to carry over and dropped the lot.
He slipped away in just a Standard Ten,
to somewhere nice like Rhos-on-Sea
while my father, who could not bid chaos welcome,
walked to the old Exchange on Lockett's Lane,
back to the 'thirties, adding up his dole.

He left behind his medical dictionary, bookmarked
and underlined in red as though every sickness
could have its understanding and solution there,
every door he barred with reasons.
But chaos, wanting no handshake or by-your-leave
always finds a way to flick aside
the goodly dreams of old Arithmetic.

SEASCAPE (FROM HOLLY'S PHOTOGRAPH)

It is a desire – among so many others – to fuse
the blue of the sky, the blue of the sea,
and the blue haze between, into an oblong
of blue, blue and blue, each part bounded
but yet relieved of its old-time dismay.

It could be said how selfish is this act
because it leaves our life behind, or out;
so intent upon the oblong, so enamoured
of its purity, we might as well be saying:
'my mother is sick and I do not care.'

Unless it could be claimed the picture is in flight,
that to the desperate eye the oblong speaks
of all discomposure, that the teeming
in all air, light, and water is also
teeming here, just lashed down in pixel or pigment.

That may be how the oblong serves a true desire.
But if it is otherwise, if it is something
merely close to what it seems,
then its leaving us aside, we dabs of people,
need not be thoughtlessly or cruelly meant.

We are finite as we stand: the workman on a roof,
the watcher on the shore. But when the silhouette
is no longer what we are, as we are shaded out,
stopped short of course of any leap to where
all circles straighten, all lines fuse,

we shall be glad – for as long as we can be –
that our mind can entertain no more
than blue, blue, and blue,
and it is by this faculty that we see where we are,
and out of what we came here, born alive.

HERE I COME

Here I come, as though
down a water-slide, head-first
from my mother's crying,
shouldering her pelvic bone, mucus-clad,
bloodied, slithering, hard to grasp,
gulping at this foreign gas,
screwed-up against the light.
Here is all there is of me,
me exactly,
into life and clinging to it
without reflection, the boundary of me,
the knuckle, kneecap,
anything there is to celebrate,
anything divine,
is here in this wawl, squirm and slather.

THE DAY BEGINS

They come into my room, these friends
whom I am always glad to see,
and insist that it is past dawn,
time to get up now.
They are bright and positive
and I am happy to hear this news
for here, lying on my back, I have been waiting
and it means I have come through.
They busy themselves about the room,
tidying, preparing,
bumping at the edges of my dream.
They are so trustworthy these friends
why would I not get up and taste the day?

NATURE NOTES

from a train:

two crows gleaning a shaven field

some dozen naked sheep nearby

I have nothing else to say on this

*

a scuffling in the undergrowth:
something wants to live unseen,
to escape notice, to make good

*

along the woodland path
this full tangle of youthful trees,
creepers, white flowers

a blotch of orange springing
from a long-fallen tree

*

its body stamped into the gravel
half-way down, printed by a tyre-track
the snake's head is intact,
its mouth open, stricken

it must have lived on like this

*

I am paused by a cobweb in the climbing-rose,
only seen in a sudden light,
awaiting the blunderers

near the light
lies the information,
the cunning architecture
of each voracious thread

*

a young fox in the headlights
turns back across the road -
the wrong choice
but it makes it

*

the yucca flowers late
its white compilations look fleecy from here
those sharp green leaves
its ramparts

on it goes

*

peaceable this whole scene
odd plots of vines, olives.
fingers of forestry, some pasture

in gray light it seems doleful
but no, leave all that behind,
just look: every single shoot intent

*

flies, specks, beetles clambering expertly
across a table or a tree
a bee heedless of its hum
a butterfly -
what can summarise all this?

*

birds of every stripe, even if at war
one with another, busy themselves
with life, will take a crumb that's offered
or leave it,
they will use our buildings
if amenable, our nooks and eaves,
our high places, but still keep their own life,
themselves to themselves,
their strange songs also constant

*

ivy dominating this patch of ground,
a thorny stick, a tree stump
flaking to pieces but fecund,
the fungi now in their season,
their pristine caps suddenly there,
brown oak-leaves among the litter,
two pale stones, a small cluster of cyclamen
all purple together

*

a vixen
(as I think)
takes her ease
in the soft dusk
close to lights

ready
but quite unhurried
even though
this is a human lawn

*

these poor leaves shaken off

once moist, rolled tight in expectation,
now crêpe beneath their tree

everything is in alteration

a pair of trousers an arthritic thumb

DISILLUSIONMENT

rain glints on the copper beech
standard cirrus motionless above

that will do –
the poem has been here
or hereabouts
many times
and what does it do
with its words?
where does it take us to?

are these rain glints
the very ones I think I saw?

disillusionment can fall
at any hour
nine eleven or twelve
just as words do
in or out of poems

remorseless
their pitter-patter

LANDSCAPE

(I)

It is not to the landscape the sadness belongs.
That is folded, mostly as we would wish,
and is steady and companionate,
its trees sheltering the special field,
that track right-angled to suit our will.
Yet sadness is part of it and so must come
from some presumption that is ours alone,
some arrogation that we depend upon.
How patiently the landscape stays with us.
Can it know how vulnerable we are?

(II)

It is a consolation for us this pleated
and slightly savage land, that and its crowded sky.
It can be claimed to be a friend, almost
as though it could converse through its clefts,
harmonise its fractured songs
and listen via the branches of its modest trees.
The harder truth is that it pays no such attention;
shelter or shade are an accidental benison.
Is there any way we can convince ourselves
that we are not ignored among the grass and stars?

(III)

I feel I have to blame the scene at large:
dark matter, distant dust, fruitful asteroids –
time – although it can no more be sensible
than any of the flowers it will not own.
It stands apart from joy and is unimpressed.
And this is why I resent its safe indifference:
how can it hold a kind of life such as
these successful shoots, water that cannot be stilled
and care for none of it at all?   ('Care'
a word we have found for ourselves hereabouts.)

(IV)

What am I saying here? Do I imply
that because there is so much around us
sturdily independent of anything we can think
or feel, there should be no cause for grief?
How small we are against approaching stars,
even against the potent busyness of worms.
Why must we want all this context
to validate us, to feel admitted by
the great unconsciousness of moss,
halting rivulets, windblown straw?

A BATCH OF FRAIL FLOWERS

a batch of frail flowers, a purplish pink,
hang close to the shadowed grass

there they are, yes just there, frail
flowers of a purplish pink

do you see that, and what do you see?
and 'shadowed grass', what do you make of that?

you might suppose it is close to dusk
as I write, though equally you might suspect
I'm clawing at consequence,
something to make the frail flowers last
into wherever they now find themselves

suddenly adjacent to thistledown
bumping against the window-pane

WALKING IN THE RAIN

Why would I go walking in the rain?
There is some gleam on surfaces
but not much for the light is faint.
The fallen leaves, lemonish and dull bronze,
cling together once gathered by the wind.
But what am I doing?
inviting melancholy, something close to solitude?
I must buy a loaf on the way home,
glad to have a project offered.

A RECTANGULAR GARDEN

At the upper right-hand corner
a large vase, terra cotta, but not an amphora,
and, just by, a palm-bush, its narrow, sharp leaves
like a comb, some of them yellow to the end,
the higher ones still a heavy green;
then, stretching along the edge, seven or eight
large stones embedded lengthways to make a border,
one pink flower remaining on the bushes there;
and I arrive at the next corner,
a grey wall of painted breezeblock,
a gap of light between every two blocks,
in fact the wall is castellated for rough effect;
light also falls on a thorn creeper that has escaped
the dense bushes clustered at the foot
of the mighty tree which is the glory of the scene;
a thin vine, whose flowers hang like catkins
about the length and colour of candles,
more than survives as it clutches the thorn,
breaking wave-like over it, winding and grasping;
where it has yet to reach the thorn-flower,
those blooms, copious and defiant pink,
look to survive deep into autumn;
coming along the third side a wooden fence,
here and there slightly mossed, some grass
pushing at the battens and planks
and two herb plots, now mostly desolate
save for some sage, parsley and tarragon,
all mis-labelled; a tap fastened to a wooden post
looks little used but ready;

this is the fourth side, the terrace bricks from which
I see all this, the curled leaves scattered
about the lawn, the upturned table I missed
in the bottom corner, its feet of gnarled and rusty iron.

*

On the paving, before the garden proper, a large
terra-cotta vase, quite empty, and behind it
a wooden fence, two metres high, and saplings
that will grow no higher, drawn up in tight array,
beside a palm, also limited, its yellowing leaves
bending earthwards; the flower-bed holds
perhaps a dozen flowers, roses possibly, all the way
to the first corner where an upturned table
lies abandoned beside a breezeblock wall,
some iron fencing a further boundary;
the tree, grand, grandiloquent even, brawny,
its bark roughcast yet still elegant, reaches
and spreads its own proportion over the garden's
leaf-strewn lawn, the tumble of bushes
that cover the wall and bound the bottom edge,
the deep pink bougainvillea, as I have learned
it is called since my previous turn, offers
great dishes of flower to a black and white butterfly
out at work; then the third side is nondescript,
just a fence against next door, a dry standpipe,
its hose looped loosely across the grass,
two herb beds enclosed by wood,
grasses rearing up the sides as though to peer
at a parsley plant, the beginnings of a sage bush
and some tarragon, fending off the weeds;

here on the bricks on the fourth side
a low divan and some cushions, still damp
from the morning rain, a straggling petunia,
its brave red flowers optimistic beneath my chair
from where there's so much to be seen:

*

The large vase, terra-cotta, but not an amphora…

PARMENIDES ON THE BOARDWALK

Out on the boardwalk today for another 'health walk'.
It keeps our feet out of the watery ground.
As usual I stop by the tree-stump decorated
with a fungus nicely confined between
splits in the wood and the curve of the bark.
A terrier passes by, as eager as ever.
Today the fungus is the pale green of a paint-chart
and is hard to the touch, plaster-like, resistant.
Is it dried and dead or in yet another phase?
If dead what was the life that has been lost?

No matter there is life everywhere,
energy in every form.
Velvet mosses clothe the bark of fallen trees;
turn up a log and shiny grubs protest at the light;
in the turbid pools the hog-louse nudges past
the ravenous nymphs of the damsel fly –
the beautiful demoiselle; leaves gleam freshly
in the reviving undergrowth; garlic

awaits its flowers; blackthorn vaunts its snowy clouds;
bacteria will be hereabouts striving furiously
as they do in yoghourt and in sourdough,
simple souls but hard as nails, their plasmids
and their daughter cells, their flagellas,
some of them, beating always towards the light.
All this comes by book or the information board
we also use to spot a bulky thrush, a robin
or that pert and fussy wren – are their 'songs'
as material as a ribosome? Another question.

Look, is that Parmenides, sandalled as we might expect,
avoiding a springer on a too-long lead?
He's valuing sense enough here,
a trip or fall would interrupt philosophy.
Further down the boardwalk that must be his goddess
waiting to accost him once again. Her cagoule is perfect.
I edge closer to listen in to what she says.
She seems to think Parmenides needs a refresher
on the One since Plato dragged it to his cave
and made of it a fashionable Idea or Form
not something solid like the ribosome.
Others, she warns, are so in thrall to the jazzy tumult
of the world they think that Reason is capsized
and Truth a mirage or a fantasy.

Poor Parmenides, you're going to have a job
getting that into your old hexameters.
Is what she's saying that the hog-louse, damsel
and bacterium are not a numbered aggregate
of different things but share something
that makes them shift and scurry, predators
and prey, and that makes them One, and us One
with them as we seize our breakfast for another day?

Parmenides shivers in the vexatious English breeze
and comes back along the boardwalk.
He nods and that gives me the nerve to speak to him.
This One, I say, *is an idea I like*
though I'm not sure why – it might be Truth.
I know it's simpler to see gnats swarming
to no tune at all, or starlings as merely particular
and not try to seek the rhyme or reason
of their gatherings.   *I hope you are going to set me straight.*
He puffs his cheeks and makes as though to speak

but then steps off the boardwalk, taking care
where he puts his foot, and disappears.
I walk on, sidling past a mastiff across the path
alert and listening for its owner's call.
The trees resume their patient climb,
the small dishes of fungus… no - too much to itemise.
The thought-filled sky absorbs it all.
I'm looking for an ending where the cadence falls.

FIRE-SMOKE

How slow this fire-smoke rising from the field.
It saunters upwards wholly at leisure
relinquishing itself contentedly enough.

This is now a morning in deep autumn,
the last leaves going but no longer plunging down,
the lights are on, the trees resolutely black
against this ancient wash-water sky.

Where is the burden here? But why translate
what comes to the eye already changed?
They did not stand a chance – 'ancient' and 'at leisure' –
they were enrolled as soon as glimpsed.

THE LUCKY TREE

To survive the winter ice the lucky tree
whose lucky seed found a post
in sympathetic ground still work
along its column's reach, draw down
into its roots all moisture and nutrition,
surrendering its leaves to the year's entropy.
The whole tree must live, its patient leaves
must flutter into death, part of the system
which we see as cruel abandonment -
Ah, the fond complacencies of metaphor!

TREES FALLING

Trees fall, of course they do,
not quite as we are taken,
but something like,
cognate, similar.

This is a verse that pleases me
but not its import:
that trees have an end
and that we follow.

So roll up your canvas rug,
imagine nothing stronger,
imagine nothing stronger than
what will fall at last.

Pack only certain clothes,
leave the rest behind.
'Rest' will prove a word
welcome eventually.

And is 'fall' another such?
(*vide* the trees above)
every kind of rug,
words on their own parade.

STANDARD MODEL

So here we find ourselves, for now,
deep in the Standard Model,
that is the way the universe is lawfully arranged
from a toilet brush to neutrinos,
though the smaller things get
the more doubtful they become,
at best a momentary smear across a screen
– was it there at all, and what does that mean?
And they, these bosons and fermions,
are everywhere, even beyond the next galaxy
and pass through everything
like a ghost through a wall –
anything but standard.
The sun on my arm, noticed briefly,

the smell of ragwort, torn and rent,
everything we are aware of
inside and outside our words
may have its bedrock in these bosons and their like
keeping us and telling us we are alive.

HERE ON EARTH

i.m. Adolfo Trippini

1

Dear Adolfo, whose joy everyday was this panorama
and your cabin in the woods
where the world was all yours, what cruelty
could make you leave it all? Salad leaves, mint,
tomatoes, sunny zucchini flowers,
strange clefted herbs, these were your province,
your own space and time
your own angolo *in which the universe*
becomes its proper size, your kitchen,
your simple garden plot, your rifugio.

2

Birds have a place in the wilderness of stars.
One alights, lurching on a branch until
it can change motion into balance,
the key to its life, just as a planet holds its steady roll.
And nearby, microbes, bacteria and other
smallest things live out their purposes

gifted from that strange fission long ago,
its bits now swirling outwards from nowhere
and cooling as gently as a bird
despite its striving to stay warm and alive.

3

The tree's slow climb is probably complete,
this is its customary canopy,
its lowest branches heavy to the ground.
Coppery its leaves, that was decided long ago
in whatever variation gave them
an advantage to intersperse regulation
avenues of dutiful poplars perfect
for guards of honour, though what came first,
the love of medals, lanyards, bayonets
or natural shuffling towards what's best?

4

The cicadas round here choose 11.30
to begin their daily chaunt, or whistle,
or clatter or whatever words have evolved
to suit their translation to our different codes.
Less than ten minutes and they quiet once more.
Perhaps the heat fails them as the breeze
disturbs whatever governs their antique limbs.
Time, moving air, the sun's warmth
might form the concert governing
the cicadas' call, utterance, rattle.

5

Grasshopper, locust, a lizard fallen
into a water pail are all part of what began
some time ago and it is their various deaths
that stipulate intervals, clock-time
and which things come last. And such
feelings as these are must have come
of what we know was rock, magma,
anyway insensate stuff. The ant's forefoot
has been seen as salvational,
such is the import of a dab of DNA.

6

The mouse escapes, out of the door, up the path
then darts left for cover, a major event
in its biography this encounter
with the human giants.
Its life is clandestine, nocturnal, bent
upon avoidance, governed by useful fear.
To us it seems no kind of life
but it shows no sign of resignation
or subservience to the wall of fate.
It has escaped and will look to flee next time.

7

This dry cistern and this tankard are 'full of life',
much of it microbial it is true
and of the kind trapped in aspic or in ice
or in Bartleby's prison yard, and all of it,
like this red speck voyaging across my page,
purposeful. Could this have been predicted?
If so when? When all was 'matter', nothing more
– scientists can find no better word –
and 'when' does not seem so useful at this distance.
My red speck has gone. It will be living somewhere.

8

Above and below, birds and fish, none of them
earthbound, ever seem to trudge
though sometimes life must feel hard –
however it was invented life *is* hard,
for elephants who must cross China,
for widows, for children by a broken water-pump.
A bowl of cherries, not! The habits of syntax
bring us to expound the counter-claim:
the sun with his hat on …his own side of the street
though it is in fact dying, no ifs or buts.

9

Life was this small leaf, detached by happenstance,
curled, yellow now overwhelming its atolls
of green. Poor leaf how I pity you.
You are only of interest now as mulch,
no more springing, no more riffling with the wind
your fond but faithless partner.   But –
that word always returns eventually –
wet mulch, a company of leaves,
will keep water in the soil meaning
a succession of leaves and more life.

10

Out there, in the 'vast rondures', light
and it seems naught else. No matter,
here we have enough to be going on with.
Look at it all! The usual ants
teeming and bustling on the subway steps,
a single snake in a hole.
What accountancy can adumbrate
a herd of deer on even one estate?
Out of what we can call nothing, all this!
and the snake giving birth in its hole.

11

Flowers are a popular sort of life,
those pinks advertising their solid shoots,
small roses, gaura riding the breeze
on their slender stems as though enjoying
their jeopardy, calling in the insects
to their tiny stars, a neat reciprocity
with the busy fly, and celandines
cushioned in the grass, their buttery yellow
belying their modesty. How we love the characters
we make of them besides the beauty of their souls.

12

Geology and gravity are here to show us where we are.
Imagine oceans falling from the basins
where they lie out into nothingness.
Imagine our little earth without its atmosphere,
no longer a handsome globe, quite contained,
but grey and knobbly, chamfered nowhere
save for the blinding salt flats, perhaps
a desert here or there. That is how it was
and the rocks strewn everywhere preserve
our history in the impress of a fern.

13

Can we count ourselves amongst the wonders of the universe?
We understand that there is a universe,
a sun and suns, stars far off from here
and how it is all molecular.
We nearly understand ourselves, not just
how to build a nest or den
but how to govern our multitudes, combat
our sicknesses, at least to within tolerances
we can accept. And the big idea:
we shall have no need of tolerances, everything will fit.

14

Or might we be an offcut or grit from
the passing gale of the universal matter
on its way to nowhere leaving us
to repine on this fretful isle, its bird-calls
the model of our own anxiety.
They call to their own, much as we are left
to do since we have realised the vacancy
about us. The wreckage that has formed
our mother earth has done well to take us
out of magma and of fire but could not sidestep…

15

To put it simply, why is there …?
Why does everything cool, as an act of nature,
A brawny ingot and a dish of tea?
What is happening to all those pieces
that left us long ago? Are they discovering
oxygen or something else that can stamp
the beginnings of what we would recognise
as life, some familiar lichen, but this time
with a permanent inscription in its cells
that forbids what we know as… death.

16

Undeniably this is a wonderful world!
For a bit broken off, graphite, dull carbon,
it has bloomed as we live it now,
convenient, congenial, hospitable even,
oxygen somehow out of light, photosynthesis,
and so, as Joseph Priestley said,
'no vegetable grows in vain'. The humble
fennel bulb, the various beans all continue
and we have something to look forward to
besides, content in the corner, Bosco the dog.

17

Apricots weaken and fall into the roadway.
They have done their job but will get
no purchase in the pounded dust
nor in the seams of paving stones.
Specks, birds and wasps, as well as us
benefit from this excess, this year anyway,
and in this part of the zone where the frost
did not claw the flowers. Is there a law,
forged deep in a capsule of the fission flare,
applying itself to this chosen tree?

18

We strive to make things beautiful,
a finial over a gateway, jasmine's
white stars climbing. We are convinced all this
will enhance the known brevity of our stay,
in some instances not only occupy but define
the time, sometimes with nature's say-so,
even with a willing partnership.
Much beauty will outlive us which is why
we press seeds into gaps and crevices.
Rock alone can never be enough.

19

Things come to seem strange as our time goes by.
This abbey for instance, its uneven stones
perfectly dressed, is enclosed now with
a kitchen-garden and a patch of vines. Beneath
the perfect proportion of campanile and church
are said to lie the bones of Syrian monks
who first brought the Word west
to Roman Umbria. Somewhere they lie,
probably in no order. What is East and West?
The compass needle shivers and tries to stop.

20

However well-chosen the spot it still makes sense
to recognise us in the knockings from
a cold tobacco-pipe, not much different
in make-up – just the matter, clinker
and common ash to be readily resumed,
drawn back into the firmament
with planets, some accelerating stars
and loose matter. Our mighty consciousness,
less than a raindrop in this company,
clings to 'mean' among its desperate words.

21

Must we celebrate this surprising globe?
It seems given to us that we should,
especially now that the blue-white entity,
seen from outside seems no more than a zephyr
curling round, drawing us to its share
of gravid force. For some, for many, for most
they find that neither grass nor gravity
is congenial. The earth has performed its tasks,
ground obdurate stuff down to silken sand,
but still there are lacks it cannot remedy.

22

Grinding is the motion that is most advanced,
mountain against mountain, the slow granulation
whether tempest or earthquake have worn
a cornice into pumice or to sand. We seize its use,
melt sand towards the most translucent glass,
talc quarried to dust a new child's skin –
nothing could be further from the granite face.
And could that be the end of us as the last bone
finds its way into a shovelful of silica
and that into a sandstorm or moveable dust?

23

This is a place where nothing grows. Nothing.
It is just a coastal sweep of sand,
empty shipwrecks, empty wind squalls.
Not a beetle climbs out of the sand,
no plasmid gets busy here or even stretches itself.
Is this how it will end or how it did begin?
Will the heat hereabouts shrivel into darkness
like a leaf drying and changing colour,
the only thing left that can change
cooling steadily towards the absolute?

24

The luck to lie out on meadow or on lawn,
absorb the mildest sun, is surely with us,
granted by the unsteady earth in its moments
of repose. With luck too we avoid
its angry shrugs, volcano, flood, tempest,
drought though these might have proved
the one condition chosen for our post.
Unless it can be shown that it is not luck
but our curacy has softened this rock
enough to bring a welcome harvest home.

25

The velvet three-note ring-dove's call
towards some other bird, is it anxious
or content? Whichever, it has its place
in the catalogue of cries, the shriek
as the owl takes its prey, the recognition
as the long-lost fulmar finds its home.
All these have been worked out, barks and cries,
suited to how they manage in this special world.
They stumble singly but still keep their kind
apprised of how to live at least for now.

26

It is easy to see this globe as a trundling
bowling-ball, nothing graceful, elegant
or light, rather a cruel rock
misshapen, palsied, its tough lianas
catching at the foot, its gales forcing us
to ground, breaking roof-trees, razing dikes,
its bilious water stretching to the sea,
its plagues finding the perfect host,
nothing discomfited to require a death
for a death, in fact requiring nothing.

PIECES OF COAL

NEW YEAR

just now
on New Year's Eve
I could not source
a lump of coal

2020 has no use
for such stuff
not even a fist-sized
chunk of the kind
that might once
have been picked
off the pit-heap
by a nine-year-old
kept off school.

a hundred years ago it got everywhere
the home-fires of Berlin
the locomotives by the Nile
Lisbon's town gas
Sweden's ironworks
the abbatoirs of Argentina
our coal
our good luck
that we could ship it
so easy to the sea
and everywhere at home
a load tipped in the entry
as the collier's ration

shovelled into fireboxes
across the nation

briquettes lit
by a gas poker
(coal gas of course)
and in fifty years
it is nowhere
finger-nails and town halls
are scrubbed clean
tips greened
into leisure walks
the coalhouse
now storage for any old thing

a piece of coal
a metonym
for fuel,
for food
for warmth
and how we need that
as the first-footer knows
from his five minutes
in the cold –
who's a lucky lad?

FLORENCE

A million-tonner
the year it was shut,
Florence pit stood
at the end of our street.
I never knew

that it was named
for this solemn, aristocratic girl,
– daughter of the third duke –

though it was he who labelled
the whole neighbourhood,
Lennox, Hamilton, Buccleuch, Rothesay
as well as Florence Primary
with its stubby tower,
slightly Italianate,
a totem for the stolid terraces,
Leveson, Gower, Blantyre and St Clair.

Nowhere in her fixes
of albumen and silver
does Florence look content.
The white cat in her lap
probably more a prop
than a pet,
the watercolour retriever
only a temporary friend.
Not for her to guest
as a gutsy Coal Queen
at the miners' picnic,
she was dead at twenty-six
of her third childbed,
a bloody mess no doubt,
not unlike the accidental agony
by then familiar
in her father's chambers
deep below
the doomed pilasters
of Barry's Trentham Hall.

SUTHERLAND'S STREETS

Sutherland's streets
have never deserved clearance.
His cottage hospital
where I was safely born
is still well-laundered,
his local library
and respected Institute,
a sore thumb three stories grand,
whose art-school windows
shimmer above
the banded brick
and handsome
terra-cotta frieze
of busy potters,
all of it symmetrical,
confident, Pevsnered.

Here my father took me
one Saturday afternoon
to get my first library card
and thereby started something:
thank you Gilbert Dalton,
A. Stephen Tring, Richmal Crompton,
and thank you
for the hush, the polish
and all the pages turned.

HEARTH

I learned to make the fire
in our grate,
newspaper, sticks,
coal-pieces smaller
than my hand
and as the yellow flame
took hold
larger pieces laid
so as to leave
the passages for draught
until our little hearth
could cast out
warmth enough
to last the evening through,
banking it with slack
so its slower burn
would leave some heat
about the room
for morning.
And so in every house like this,
thankful for coal's precious shine,
its smoke of welcome,
habitation, life.

*

This was the time we knew
the glaucous character
of phlegm,
the smoke's particulate sludge,
hawked up and blown
expertly at a sullen coal,

the stuff of dust disease
drooling from old men's
lips as they stop to lean against a wall.
And still
the lazy smoke
and gentle heat rises
through cooling towers,
furnaces and flues
to coddle the planet
in its fatal shawl.

TRIP ADVISOR AND THE DIGLAKE DISASTER

for William Cooke

Field and copse,
genteel English greenery
the roots still feeling their way through
the last shreds of motte and bailey.
The top tip for things to do hereabouts
is the multi-coloured climbing-wall,
or a brass-rubbing of the warrior boss.

Not much-remarked
the 'nearly 80', or 83, or 73 –
78 names are on the stone
though one is chiselled twice,
so 77 though only 3 are buried here
in the Wesleyan churchyard.
The rest lie somehow,
chambered inside the softened land:
19 in the new ten foot,

40 in the East seven foot,
12 in the West eight foot,
and the boy Alfred Hodgkinson,
on his own,
perhaps by the Gauge Door.

EMPIRE NEWS

'What rogues the English are!'
Naguib Mahfouz, *Palace Walk*

OCEAN ISLAND

HMS *Ocean*, touring the Southern Seas, happened by in 1800
and Banaba, though just a speck at 6 square kilometres,
barely worth the Empire's tallying, became Ocean Island.

Until 1900 when the chemists found phosphate, soon super-phosphate
and the British Phosphate Commission risked £50
on a nine hundred year lease and fertilised Australia till 1979.

By then the Banabans had had to leave their scraped-out isle
for somewhere near to Fiji some 2000k away.
A few still dream of a return to their sacred caves
but with the topsoil gone, the island stripped, lowered towards flood
what could otherwise be done, to what could they return?

The commissioners left only their mildewed swimming pool,
        their dead machines and did not re-plant a single tree.

The London court allowed a 'moral debt' was owed.

THE BEDFORD DOWNS MASSACRE

'Shooting time is all done with in the Kimberley,
        he can have a life here in the cattle.
        His name Goo-woo-something unpronounceable,
        he'll not need that, I'll call him Paddy after me.
And for his other name, for the books,
        why not Bedford, he is a lad from hereabouts,
the hilly pasture, much like Dunstable back home.
And to give him another bit of English
        he could learn to drive the truck,
        the old two-ton Bedford barrelling
        down the roadway, a real Luton bloke.'

*

And so he was for sixty years, a stockman
        tinkerer and roadman at Bedford Downs
        where the cattle trod and trod, packing
        and pressing the ground till nothing grew there,
        the emu, bush turkey, cockatoo
        even the rainbow-serpent just roadkill.

*

Paddy made this, 'The Bedford Downs Massacre',
    and it is a painting not a story,
    the deep red is all it is, 'the hand of art'
    representing nothing.   *Terra nullius.*

A story is in time, a history, the Bedford Downs Massacre 1921
    for us is a history and it passes.
    For Paddy there is no time, it is not a history.
    It is here, stationary, in his mind and in the paint.

SUEZ

De Lesseps and his million men did the spadework
    and then it was up to us.   As when:

the imperial pigeon-shooters set off
    yet another incident and the natives just don't see
    that this is sport, only sport, why do they make such a fuss
    over a pigeon-pie?
So we have to hang this Egyptian lad in front of his own house,
    and his own mother,
    and take the lash to a good many more.
It will be long remembered.

And so it was.
Though fat Farouk in his fez was at least a pal we could recognise,
    Big-Nose harboured such things.
    He had his snout in the cut from the start and it was lost
    and all our khaki sands were through the glass and gone.

A RESPECTABLE LIFE (NOTES FOR AN OBITUARY)

Henry, a decent English gent. for sure,
all the way from his knickerbockers
in the 1840s to 1923, a safe M.P.,
Chancellor of the Duchy for a year in 1885,
always a man of neckties, monocles and means.
Jilted in 1855 (she ran out the back of Marshall and Snelgrove
into a carriage and her lover's arms), he married Lady Florence,
but never again after she died in her third childbed.
Perhaps it was a grief he never could assuage,
or possibly, because he had sons in hand,
he had no further need to bother.
It was this Henry gave his name to our not-quite-arterial,
far from imperial Chaplin Road, our way to the Alhambra,
Storm over the Nile, Gunga Din, the better man
unrecognised in our fellow-citizens
who have made Dr. Heslin's sturdy house a serviceable mosque.
Was that an accommodation Henry could have sought?
To summarise:
Henry Chaplin, unexceptionable parliamentary commoner
of our commonweal, faithful widower, owner
of a Derby winner, eventual Viscount,
banked all his life the steady dole of reparation

won for his career and comfort by his father, the Reverend Henry,
ex-owner of a far-off family of Grenadan slaves.

'THE COMPANY-STATE'

Did Lady Clive's ferret wear its diamond collar
when set at large in Shropshire warrens
or was it too much of a pensioner by then
for country sports, lank and slack
on its cushions, fed on caramels?

Leadenhall Street may have looked askance,
thinking only their grey ledgers
were the proper instruments of wealth
but what's the difference after all?
However austere *seth, shaff* and counting-house
they all dealt in loot, loot, loot.

Milord Vulture, Diamond Pitt, building docklands
buying boroughs, 'shaking the pagoda tree'
down the generations, ancestral easements
school fees, little luxuries stashed from afar.

The mahout tumbled to the ground however caparisoned.
The sepoy learned to keep his powder dry.

THE EMPRESS OF INDIA

Queen Victoria does not look too comfortable
in her cartoon howdah.   The elephant
looks knowing, the mahout, if not mutinous,
is at best impassive, the scotch bonnet all eyes.
And the queen is feeling the lurch and is holding on.
For all our efforts Indians will not yet
become Englishmen and perhaps they never will.

In the Durbar Room at Osborne House sits a statue of
Ganesh, popular god who likes sweets
and is said to move whatever gets in the way.
At his foot sits an obedient rat,
tail neatly curled, waiting for permission
to satisfy his undoubted appetite.
He is the type of continence, governance
of desire – in fact he could be English!
He understands that famine, like our rule, is Providence.

That we have not taught their own god's commandment well
makes us half ashamed.

THE KENYA EMERGENCY

'Yes, Mr Howlands was coming to enjoy his work.'
Ngũgĩ Wa Thiong'o, *Weep Not Child*

What is Emergency? Is it inhuman deeds?
Many wonderful tortures? Where does
custration come from? Is that the democratic law?
Is this the British system or the Nazi system?

Castration with barbed wire? Surely not sir,
not our kind of thing at all. Not even for the Mau Mau.
Stout gloves and pliers maybe,
our man on the spot knows the situation best.
We are driven close but not near to sin.
Our civilising mission: MMBA, miles and miles of
bloody Africa.

'weasels fighting in a hole' to quote-unquote one of their very own,
some bard or other, and that's how we Britishers see the
Irish plain:
1798 scrabbling after the French; Fenian bombs and bastards;
Black and Tans; Enniskillen; Warrenpoint;
Ballymurphy, poor drear Armagh and its murder mile;
the fancy butchers of the Shankill Road.

But there is Gaelic Guinness and the *craic*,
horses, jockeys, Irish jokes and squeezebox singalongs,
St Paddy's Day when Brit expats in Singapore wear
stovepipe hats in emerald green
and drunk as leprechauns toast some great-grandad
who may have hailed from Connemara long ago.

A touch of Irish license once a year's our due,
we who ever since the Anglo-Normans, Strongbow
and Mountjoy, Cromwell and his crew have fought
to bring some tidiness and industry to
these 'barbarous wretches' and their crackpot land.

It's ours, a British isle we'll not surrender,
unless, that is, it proves more trouble than it's worth
and they vote to leave us and sink beneath the waves.
By Jove we'll drink to that we will.

COVERDALE

From a train, as so often noticed, the backside of the city:
Dead motors, fly-tips, tyre-dumps, unclaimed rubble,
        sunless repair shops, any old iron.
Amid this, its grass surrounds striving to stay spruce,
        the Coverdale Baptist Church, eccentric in Ardwick,
        built to be different in 1970, Ernest Geoffrey Seddon,
        architect, now part of Eddie's twentieth century;
Good, careful brick and plentiful glass built to promulgate
        the ghostly psalms.

How amiable are thy dwellings thou Lord of Hosts!
Yea, the sparrow hath found her an house and the swallow
        a nest where she may lay her young

*

Nothing amiable in the end about Fort Ardwick, or Fort
        Beswick, nor any of Hulme's royal crescents,
        the 70s systems built to solve the problem of the poor.
Their old lavatories down the yard (that fearful drop), fitful
        gas mantles, cold clinker in the hearth of a morning,
All that needed clearing and how different, how systematic
        this all looked,
Pueblos of progress but soon leaking, crumbling,
        so much shoddy.
And the poor were spilt there.

And the systemisers were confounded:

God thou knoweth my simpleness, and my faults are not
        hid from thee.

Let not them that trust in thee, O Lord God of Hosts be
ashamed for my cause...
for thy sake I have suffered reproof; shame hath
covered my face...

(This time they/we are trying to do better.)

*

But Coverdale's church, the plaque to the Glory of God
hidden by weed-stalks,
stands undefeated: drums, vocals and bass guitar are lifted up;
volunteered furniture fills the nave, a clutter of dressers,
beds, settees and chairs, no doubt other stuff, a kettle
pots and pans,
each re-claimed, re-made, re-purposed.
And reaching across the kitchen-counter and trestle-tables,
the cooks, the servers, outside the gardener, the sweepers-up
and here too the totters-up making the ends meet.

These shall not be defeated.
Not by the girl shooting up into her eyeball,
not by half-taught plutocrats,
not by the shit-stained drunk,
not by the hedge-fund pensionaries,
not by the battered, not even by the batterer,
not by all those enjoying their desserts,
not by she who cannot care,
not by the comfortable like yours truly.

For the poor shall not always be forgotten; the patient
abiding of the meek shall not perish for ever.

ANTIQUE CAMELIAS

How much my mother
would have loved
these strange flowers,
their rich petals,
their decorous pink,
though there were none
in our garden,
only aubretia
modestly satisfied,
roses bought by post,
pansies, gawky lupins
shaking themselves.

At one time
there were brambles,
gooseberries, thistles
and dock, hiding-places,
though that space was not ours
until it was bought
so rental garages
would not be built
too close.

Down to the line-post
the garden was for
Monday drying,
sheets and shirts,
the smell and steam,

soap and starch,
the corrugated tub,
the wooden dollypeg –

domestic security,
nothing bought from afar.

My mother and father
came from yards
not gardens,
yards with a lav.
like a brick sentry-box,
cold, newspaper
on a nail,
all to be left behind,
a garden was better
even if the soil
was gravelly,
nasturtiums
making their way through cinders,
but a lawn
was grass
sometimes to be
sat out on,
a deckchair
another new thing
like the mower
so carefully
and regularly oiled.

All this a prospect
from the scullery
and from the table
every day.

MUG AND JUG

a self-portrait without a face
just his blue trousers, white shirt
and tooth-mug

an empty table-cloth, blood-red,
fills the room, I repeat, blood-red and
fills the room

a red boat melting on the water

a man suddenly falling over

shaded silence: enamel plates,
a tall jug

out of some things that can be listed:
sacking, iron, plastic, tar,
cellotex, scrap, often partly burnt

these are of sufficient interest

sadly I want them to lead me elsewhere

BACON'S DOG

anxious or angry
turning and turning
perhaps on a swatch of lawn
its fierce snout pointed at the ground
its teeth glaring but useless
this dog is suffering somehow

cars pass by on the roadway,
beyond that is the line of the sea
then an unhelpful sky

TWO PIANOS

i.m. Roy Fisher

I am listening to Renato Sellani (piano)
who has the softest touch,
sometimes so close to silence.
Sellani at lunchtime, the gnome
of 'My Funny Valentine',
the sun strong through the window,
his cigarette smoke hanging in its light.

And I am put in mind of an old friend
confined to his chair, looking at
Earl Sterndale in the mirror above his mantelpiece.
He can see enough from there he says.
He paid attention.

The thing about them both is the piano,
for Roy that and poetry,
the codes of rhythm.
To their innermost of course I was not privy.

DID I REALLY DO THIS?

All my life I have insisted
that I really did walk out of school
on my very first day, my very first morning.

Yes, it is true. I just left the classroom
when the teacher's back was turned
and walked out and home,

three-quarters of a mile across a road
admittedly less busy than it is now
to reach our street and arrive

at the top of our path and see my mother
look up astonished from the kitchen step
she was scrubbing clean on hands and knees.

I had looked forward to the nursery sandpit,
its lorries, tipper-trucks and cars
but they had moved me next door to desks and sums.

In the afternoon I was reconciled:
I did not want a smock and a baby-sleep
but to join the world: pullovers and pencils.

All true, I insist, and how well I remember
most of it, though what does it mean,
does it belong in the story I have to tell?

PERCE

Perce!   Hey Perce!   Wait!

I've been trying to catch you all my life!
Wait a minute.
I'd just like a word.

You'll not know me
but I'm your nephew
I was here before you were gone,
you wouldn't know.
I'm your replacement sort of.

Look, I'll be quick.
It's a good photo that you left,
smart, smiling, hair nicely combed,
you look friendly,
was that you?
that sort of lad?

All my life I've tried to catch you.
Don't be a stranger

or this ghost.
I've had to make you up
from the photograph

and having your name,
still laughable Percy,
and here you are –
you might pause and look at me
and wonder who –

'what's this lad want of me?'

But you must get on,
your greatcoat's gone
and now in your tropical kit,
you've got your death to deal with.

You turn away
back into the photograph –
I couldn't replace you
for all the years I've had,
and you weren't born to be a memory.

Why should you stop,
look over your shoulder even?
You're there now
and I've nothing for you.

THE SHADES

they look up
for a moment
their attention drawn
and nod and note

that their niece
has followed them
just this afternoon
–how could that be
how could it be her time?

but they know just how
and that it is

they are not much occupied
no sweeping
nothing novel
no surprise

their footprints
do not stray far
their hems and
trouser cuffs
trail in the dust
dried nosegays
no more than sticks
are shuffled
from one hand
to another

they have nothing to say

they do not wish
or watch
or wait or greet
the boulder is neither
shelter nor feature

she takes her place
a small way off

the most they do
is know

THE WINDOW AGAIN

How often do I come to this window?
Outside, on a step at eye-level, a hefty
long-lived pot-plant, its leathery leaves
doing their best against autumn.
Behind that, tidy brickwork, its mortar now going
black in places, though only slowly
and with what looks like
some beginnings of moss.
This wall cuts out of sight all but some branches
and foliage of the confident trees beyond,
another year – leaves
and bare branches, their regular cycle.
To the left, in the right-angle of the window-frame
a clear patch of sky, just now a thin grey
that continues through the shifting gaps in the branches.
And that's it, as much as there is to be seen,
parts of things.   At night I draw the blind.

INTERVAL

Did you just give up and go,
decide that seventy-odd was fair-dos
and anyway you'd had enough
of pills, scans and what you can't remember?

All that stuff in envelopes and biscuit tins,
photos that deserved another look
will have to take their chances now,
you couldn't deal with everything.

May those of us most likely to be missing you
get past that and live our life.
You won't want to spoil one day of what's
left to us since we were pushed out here
into this interval that always ends
before it's finished but has to do.

HERE I GO

Here I go, no, not 'here I go again',
but here I go the once, the only time,
the approaching final second, that moment,
no other, no second chance as
inside this boundary there is less and less
able to marshal its chemistry
against this change,
less and less of this life
that only knows that it is life that it wants,
life that it wants.

AN AFTERLIFE

In his best suit,
dark brown, pin-striped,
he is ready for that perfect peace,
quietly laid down forever,
except that he finds himself
surrounded
by a dozen or so men,
also brown-suited,
hempen prisoners of eternity
yet all of them chortling,
jostling the newcomer
neither listening to his name
nor betokening friendship of any kind,
nothing made of the old life,
then leaving him
and he knows he must follow,
join this bustling of the spirit world
in some nearby perpetual corner,
no sign of what they once searched for,
the oblivion they always expected
and even dreamed of.

STILLNESS

Stillness. Only a bird moves in sight,
the flack of its wings, hurrying.
But the rest of the landscape
seems motionless - distant towns,
houses apart rust-red or cream in colour,
swathes of woodland hiding so much,
empty yellow fields,
the white stretch of warehousing,
a church steeple poking out of the green,
there is rough land, cultivated trees,
purposeful roads and tracks seemingly unused.
A single white boat breaks the lake.

TO HENRY VAUGHAN

Ascension Day again! and you as cheerful
as on Whit Sunday and all the other
holy-days on which you can rejoice,
but not along the prom prom prom
where the brass band goes tiddly om pom pom.
and the Big Dipper whoops and swoops

But that is how it is nowadays,
Sangria and Solaire, many of us
worldlings laughing in the light
that we see shining hereabouts,
dancing pom pom, delighting pom pom
in every shimmer of our sequinned clay.

You could write these poems every day
celebrating your Lord's beneficence
or lamenting how you find yourself remiss,
your mind filled with God and his worthy son,
nailed into your imagination,
surely a dull engagement even then.

We have reasoned our way to candyfloss
and penicillin pom pom. Given up your way
of seeing the world (or worlde), happy
to be busy and restless both in work
and precious play, content to see no meaning
in this battered frame … om pom, om pom, om pom, om pom …

… OR POSSIBLY A PARASOL

after Peter Doig, 'Lapeyrouse Wall'

(1)

A man under an umbrella,
or possibly a parasol,
his hat clapped on
walking beside a wall,

is walking somewhere
in the universe
specific to his needs,
but no less a part of it all

occupying some space
just as an invisible star does,
what happens on that star,
or like an atom of hydrogen,

or the sun beating
on the polka dots
or the pink of his parasol,
another detail he belongs with.

(11)

A man under an umbrella,
or possibly a parasol,
now in a brilliant shirt
clean white no sweat stains

is quite specific
separate from anyone
in a canoe
or a prison cell.

His trousers flap
even in this slight breeze
and from behind it's hard
to tell he wears glasses.

All in all
there isn't anything
in the universe
compiled as he is.

(III)

A man under an umbrella,
or possibly a parasol,
walks along the pale wall
lit by what we all know

to be a part of us,
a part that is visible
and that enables us
as it does this man

making his way through
the shadows cast
by the lamp standard
the fire hydrant

the far-off mountain
and other things
that comprise
the present universe.

(IV)

A man under an umbrella,
or possibly a parasol,
out here taking the air,
breathing it in.

oxygen has met him here
though he thinks little about it
especially not
how strange it is,

how rare it might be
in the whole universe,
one element
which helps him

walk past the prison wall
along the pavement
past the hydrant
and onwards.

(v)

A man under an umbrella,
or possibly a parasol,
perhaps thinks as he walks,
perhaps of a son who works

in a different country
far away who has not
found a partner yet
and postponed a visit yesterday.

Or he thinks how strange
to find this street
suddenly unfamiliar,
the kerb and the lamppost

parts of a world he knows,
but for a few moments
utterly unknown,
some kind of elsewhere.

(VI)

A man under an umbrella,
or possibly a parasol,
has the street to himself,
maybe on every day

if it is early morning,
though can the sun
be so strong
he needs a parasol?

The whole universe
has questions such as these
(it is not raining)
and he walks through problems

while knowing that
he takes the same road
in the same shoes
never skipping.

(VII)

A man under an umbrella,
or possibly a parasol,
walks gravely
towards the future

as though it is
always there,
changing a little
day by day

in ways that are
easily acceptable
but is not in fact
the true future

which is quite different
with no interest
in his height
or his precious hat.

(VIII)

A man under an umbrella,
or possibly a parasol,
walks beside the prison wall
admitting some words

into his mind
glass honour aptitude,
not a sequence that would
incriminate him in the town.

A cliff where the path
starts to rise
looks blue to his eye,
or so it seems –

but who can guess
another's apprehension
whether stranger
or familiar?

(IX)

A man under an umbrella,
or possibly a parasol,
stays largely
unperturbed by

the news that
our universe,
as estimated,
might one day or second

dissolve in a single flash
taking all his thoughts
and moods,
our theories

and our laws
into the same
flat oblivion
as his useful parasol.

AFTER WALLACE STEVENS

Out in the garden summer has become autumn.
autumn is becoming winter, youth is getting old.

A bus caught in traffic shuts off and waits.
Birds fly past, their urgency more than evident.

Grass is often to be found in poems…
Let's stop there, pretend that is enough.

Are there 'many meanings in the leaves'?

CRUEL WORLD

It's mostly cruel here,
fire flood and plague
the famous catalogue,
even birds, free as they are,
have it tough,
owls thwarted by the rain,
predators, frequent lack.

We make the best we can,
flowers helped along tenderly
soften the brutish scene,
take our minds off
put them elsewhere
as for a holiday,
and jaunty lights

strung between trees cheer
whoever can come out tonight.

From somewhere
all of this must seem comical
as we forever cock an ear
for danger or for promise,
always expecting,
always looking
for a smudge of smoke
on the horizon
and a good captain
honour-bound to send
a cautious boat ashore.

OF LIFE: NOTES

do you find life
all it's cracked up to be?

going on
something like this:

the crucial drip of acids
out of rock or clay

rough existence
near trees

the nous to hide
and run away

sharing
and so many rules

devised to ease
time together

time
such an invention -

artificial light
techne of every kind

the raw and the cooked
the painting of bison – why?

consciousness
without mirrors

gilt or otherwise
me and others

eventual relish
clitoral pleasure

and similar
diversions

thought disinterested
beyond easy boundaries

the idea of death
knowing it

grief grievance
grieving

life defined
by nothing so much as its end

QUIET

Quiet. Nothing to be heard.
Far below a truck comes from nowhere
and disappears.
The silence seems alien, aggressive,
unwilling to give any quarter.
Something rolls across the cobbles,
trolley-like. It seems comforting,
at least for the moment. It completes
what may be its task and then perhaps
someone steals away without a footstep
or the slightest cough.
Silence in sunlight resumes.

AMORES

Publius Ovidius Naso, playful
Roman poet, saw it all start like this:
the earth nothing but winds and matter,
neither form nor liquid, shapeless, raw,
not even the stars above, no sun

and so no moon, nothing seen or to be seen.
How did this change to allow the arts of love,
all that Venus brings, the precious details
of her labile gifts, her bracelets of attention,
our finger-tips taught to amaze us?

CUPID WEEPS

One of us must go
and Cupid's bow will be broken.
He will drag his feet,
beat his breast
all along Victoria Road,
his happiness and ours
once completed at 135,
tangled at his bidding
on an afternoon divan.

O Cupid do not weep.
We have been grateful
for your marksmanship
and Venus' sweat
these sixty years.
Calmness awaits.
It must be the time
for us to learn
the kind declutch
of philosophy

But is there such a thing?
A thought capable

of accepting the loss
of the excitement
of each others' hands
across our bodies
as they go?
There is no consolation
in any words usable.
That is why Cupid weeps.

DRAGGED AWAY

Dragged away, all of us, sooner or later,
dragged away under the toils of chemo, cardiac stoppage,

hunger, thirst, weariness or whatever, like
cirrus combed about the sky, widening

and dissolving, meeting at last the lake-shadow
whose darkness takes us beneath its clouded coverlet.

We leave thinking of what life has been, the best parts of it,
and of all we cannot know, would not have known

even if we had been granted hours enough
to pick our way beyond this thicket of bemusement.

Everything there is, fruit trees, fir forests, fields of wheat
is waiting in its obvious, patient beauty

for its own demise, however slow and beyond us.
A town on the far hill, busy and unconscious,

the drivers crawling down the motorway cannot pause
to think of their incredible ending, their loss

of everything that has been familiar and unknown,
the future closing in as we all so nearly recognise.

THE INVENTION OF THE SOUL

O my soul, where are you?
Easy to find in Florence County Primary
and the Church of the Resurrection Sunday School,
something comforting like a woollen doll
or a small cloud lodged in the breast.
But you've been gone a long time,
playing hide and seek with the anatomists
as they chopped and searched, glad,
it seems, that what they cannot see or feel
in this universe of ours does not exist.

The Philosopher – though which one we may ask –
looks at himself and sees life, sense and reason.
Pull them together and we have the bodily soul.
The fly hurrying across my page
leaping as we cannot,
or the horse shitting where it will
giving joy to a thousand flies,
these have life, and some sense, as for instance
the danger for the fly of some interruption
of its settled path, or the thunderflash
that makes the horse throw its tolerated rider.
But they cannot reason as we can,

fix a pole into the ground to help a vine
or other plant reach towards the sky.
The rational soul learns how to plant the earth.
Is that what the soul is, ingenuity?

And can we therefore give ourselves eternal life?
Because Copernicus figured out
the earth goes round the sun,
does it mean my mother was right
that she would meet my father after death?

As the body teeters towards dissolution,
and finds its final hiding-place
or sheds all but its bones until they calcify
into powder in the voracious air,
so we must invent something that will survive,
The various souls may fill the bill.
They are convivial enough it seems,
ascending from this clumsy body
in no shape that we can understand
but indestructible, ready to find friends
old and new, companionate for eternity,
eventually, perhaps, restored to bodily perfection.
The reason I wish this old tale were true
is that my mother was not disappointed by her end.

But none of this will be found by Dr Tulp,
the brain opened to its grey enthusiasm,
even the modern ferreting of this
mysterious mechanism of dendrils
and the rest, that mish-mash, will not reveal
a blessed centre, the hollow residence we seek.

Suppose there is nothing to be sought,
that death is what it appears to be
and has been since what we call life
happened out of this planetary coincidence.
The soul is only what it needs to be.

CASUALTY

My manikin model,
for art purposes
articulated
ankle knee and neck,
lies on my desk
half on his back
one arm curiously
stretched into the air
his elbow bent backwards
his featureless face
towards the sky
as though beseeching.

Could a genuine corpse
have this rigidity,
or would its elbow
long ago have
dropped to the ground
alongside the body?
The rigour
holding them,
woodenly at first,
softens

then deliquesces
from the sharp wound
outwards
if not gathered in

Each one like
my manikin
brings to mind
a man of bone and muscle,
limbs once useful
now splayed,
unable to carry
the munitions box,
lips closed
on a tree root
not on his lost canteen.
He is ordinary,
never more than now,
no longer one
who was recognized
by several neighbours
who will mourn him
particularly, resolutely,
as long as
they can bear it,
leaving him at length
to those who sent him here,
the well-dressed,
and well-wrapped,
their as yet unsplintered
regiments like him,
wooden numbers
styled to stand
or run

or wave,
each joint available
until they trip
and fall
torn like paper
arms legs improbable

even in art.

DISTANCE

such a grand universe
we have, forever grander

material
beyond our ken

beyond this mind
of ours

lightless stuff
strange rays

everything
there is

*

we think we can
observe,

that we are at
some vantage point

from which
we can see

each small
discoloration

fading
'out there'

*

we are so much
it seems,

out of dust
so remarkable

whippoorwills
in space

'space' a word
like 'whippoorwill'

and which we can call
remarkable

*

words, it is
all of it words,

useful as they are
they will expire,

syntax, also something
we have made

will fall apart,
its gravities,

its lonely pressures
overcome

*

all of it words,
we try

to make them
stick

but what is
'out there'

won't have them,
what can they do

for the universe
which requires nothing?

*

but we need to have
what might be called

a ledge or a line
somewhere or there is

no sense to it
only light

that cannot arrive
or explain itself

nothing but
distance

ELEMENTAL

Death, as I have said before,
is what it appears to be,
plants tell us so

their weariness
as their leaves
go brown
their flowers
droop

they came about
as this strange planet
made up
what is called
life

and what is that?
a cheetah
running down
a weakened antelope

two men
chattering

so many other things

life the pre-requisite
for death

death like life
is something happening.

EXCESS

One lies
drenched in thought.
The human is excess
of consciousness.
Robert Gray, 'After Heraclitus'

So are trees, for instance, happy things,
content to live as they do,
even when the wind
strips their branches,
their countless seedlings
fall without issue,
their girth
overcomes them
so that they must fall
to the whirr
and careful curacy
of their surgeon's hands?

As the rain falls
they are drenched,
especially if
it comes in stair-rods.
'Drenched', 'stair-rods',
two words often used
in our house
when caught in a downpour:
'drenched' a thorough soaking,
complete, physical;
'stair-rods' as though

there is no let-up,
the raindrops seem all
joined together in a single
straight line downwards
and hard.

'Drenched in thought',
Robert, you tell us how we are,
unavoidably.
So would we rather
be a tree,
or a lake,
or a rusty garden fork
unconscious of its use,
not unhappy
as we frequently are
in our 'excess
of consciousness'
in which we only sometimes
achieve the composure,
the indifference
of a tree, a lake,
a garden fork,
everything that surrounds us.

'Drenched',
'stair-rods',
may they tell us how we are –
'words',
a part of the 'excess'?

FELLOW CREATURES

1.

Good morrow brother lizard,
here we are again,
us and the walking fly,
born to exist a while
not far from harm.
Harm is what you expect
and why you stop, attentive
as always, a pulse of breath
by the stone in the threat-filled air.

Shall I call you brother
because we all came here
as protons seeking rest,
bumped daily by neutrinos
passing by? Is this enough
to make us brotherly,
you and I and the walking fly?

2.

For Saint Francis – have you heard of him? –
this is more than enough.
For him the birds were Creation's choir,
the slug underfoot
a recipient of love,
the slightest ant,
and you the lizard and the fly,
had its projects respected.

Ah Saint Francis, the paragon
of us all, determined
to do no harm,
to spite no one,
not even those who wear the softest clothes.
Given that he was granted
a life to live, to exist a while,
he listened to its choices
and then chose service
of the leprous and the lame.

Was he not a model for all men,
a man not a god
who might show us how we might become
generous and benign?
Yet how could he not believe
the boar or wolf might turn on him.
That Christian hearts,
swanking in their siege towers,
could before his eyes
kill the 80,000 souls
of Damicetta, those
who survived the siege
butchered in the street,
parents raped and enslaved,
fear waiting forever for
an arena of revenge.
O brave lizard, thoughtless fly
Can this organism live otherwise?

3.

Out of so many, many
years of light
has all this come.
Insensate particles
binding and huddling,
finding a form at last
out of the ocean,
struggling like tadpoles,
legs afoot,
until they reached
philosophy.

4

And, brothers,
we have reached it,
textbooks for the Good:
do unto others…

Born to exist a while,
we try to live
the thoughts we've made.
We try, but at the last,
if pressed enough
by hunger, comfort,
the corporal's command to shoot,
we are but breathing creatures
avoiding harm.

LOOK!

Look! here it is again,
well, not again,
it is always here,
that cabbage-y plant,
holding its corner,
its bottom leaves now
wholly brown and curled,
the sturdy upper leaves
edged and eaten brown
but otherwise so green, clustered,
the light from inside,
a reflection
doubled by the glass,
hangs just above it,
against the brick.
That's enough,
leave it alone.

NO PHILOSOPHER

'I'm no philosopher,' says she
'I like this life too much, I just do',
and she stands outside Tesco
with a trolley-load, piles of tins,
frozen meals, chocolate desserts, dog-food,
Cokes family-size, New Zealand wine.
She wants to cling to what she has
not go seeking other worlds,

abstractions and the like as she once did,
hidden truths always somewhere else,
nowhere near the Tesco carpark that's for sure.
And death always hanging around
forever expecting to be solved
as the soul jumps clear of the body
to live on in its perfect realm
free from the smell of Glade and cabbage.
To think, she says, I was once wrapped up in all that,
trying to look up, always up
and not looking where I put my feet
treading dog-shit into the house.
How did we ever come to think
experience is not real?

She scans the entrance looking for Jay
and his 4x4 coming to collect her and the shop.

She's stranded with not much else to do but think
which she's barely done for years,
not since that finals class with Mike
who showed her what metaphysics could be
to someone who was a shopgirl two years before.

Socrates' mother was a midwife,
but even so she still thinks he was a rum old bugger,
managing to die happy because his soul is free,
the whole world and its storecard points
'dematerialised' into the eternal.
So the remedy for death is death
which doesn't get us very far,
and as for the dream of reason
and the hope of justice both disappointed,
well of course they are,

and now it's coming on to rain,
he'd better get here in a minute.
And this wind as well,
not the wind of thought, oh no,
I should have brought a coat.

She tries to push her trolley undercover
but one of its wheels has just got jammed
and is hard to move. Is this
what they meant by 'Being?' she wants to know
as the wheel turns sideways
and resists a kick from her newest pumps.
No it's only appearance, the way things
seem to be, inconvenient, noticeable
like birth with its blood and mess
but not important and soon forgotten
for higher thoughts and things.
I liked these pumps now look at them.

She struggles with her phone but Jay's
not picking up. She'd call an Uber
but you need a password, yes?

Where is Jay? Did he get the girls from Gym?
He can do his bit now – he stuck it out
in the labour ward, looking for any chance
to feel excluded but always a help.
He picks the girls up, remembers
their Coke and favourite snack,
tries to notice what they are wearing.
He knows that none of us will live forever,
that it's all downhill like when he had to
give up five a-side last year – there's

Philosophy for you, Man and mutability! –
that procreation is the best that we can do.

Here comes another Ford Fiesta to collect
a woman and her stuff. Come on Jay
you can't leave me here thinking.

Philippa and Lizzie, both good kids,
polite to their grandparents, do their homework
every night. What will they make of us?
Will they realise that everything they are,
every thought they take has its origin
in the chance of me and Jay getting together?
That's what it follows from, like me,
in the meeting of mum and dad
one night by the sound-desk they said,
and so on backwards,
back and back and back?

'Poor Reason' amid that much chance,
'a child angered by tiredness that will not sleep.'
I can see that alright.
Our Lizzie was a terrible sleeper
but now she's top in Maths.
'Reason seeks an ending' but also loves endlessness,
wants to close things up, or down,
but then says an argument can have no ending.
That's Lizzie all over, arguing the toss,
never giving in. Jay says she takes after me.
God help her teachers, she must be a nightmare
to have in class. What would – or will
she make of Hegel and the causality of history,
eliminating free will. She'll not have that –

‘the unfreedom of the human mind’ and
‘the compulsions of nature’, not likely,
her and her purple hair, bless her.
She’s an understander. But suppose it can’t be done,
that we must live with the impossibility of truth,
does that mean we cannot be at home
in the world, never could have been?
So what’s her Dad up to?

He’s a good half hour late now.
How would it be if we had no concept of time?
If we had no concept of change, nor past
present and future and that all we had had to do
was keep things the way they’ve always been.
I made a note about this and
Australian Aborigines
but Jay’s nothing like them
unless he’s changed a lot this morning.

It’s belting down now and getting cold as well.
Why do we care about that so much?
It’s only material after all.
A daft question.
The truth is that’s the way we are,
ontologically speaking. We’ll not get past it.
Phil and Lizzie can do a salto
on the vault but only defy the earth
for a moment. They can’t stay aloft
no matter how good their spring
and the landing has to be just right.
No transcendence in gymnastics
whatever it looks like!
Even if they learn the Yuschenko
they won’t be able to do it forever

but will stumble into death
probably not getting the landing right.

Enough of that, I've forgotten the hand-wipes again
I'm not going back now. Jay doesn't use them anyway.
I forgot them. Am I responsible?

I stopped worrying about the Good Life years ago.
My dissertation on it was good
but what did that amount to?
Is this the Good Life, being able to fill
this trolley, buy the girls new leotards,
have it off with Jay once or twice a week.
That's *eudaimonia* for you!
But there has to be more to it than that.
We've taken on these girls and they must live
virtuously. They'll not learn that by reasoning,
or by looking after #1,
they'll learn by acts, what we do and what
they learn to do. What I thought about
and wrote about is still busy round the back.

I could do wrong, there's plenty of chance at work.
So sometime could the girls,
and Jay though he'd sleepwalk into it.
But he'd be ready to take the rap,
not think that since the universe is silent
he could get away with it, no one
and nothing to notice and judge
what he has done, or left undone
what he ought to have done.
I made him give up church when he met me
so he probably won't think about it
this way, but he knows he should live

as though there's judgement waiting.
But what's judgement, what's virtue?
The trouble starts with the nouns.

What do I think? Even Plato and
Aristotle believed we could get it right
eventually, that we could perfect Reason
at least enough to make sense of life, understand
how we can live here as we would want.
But there are others, literary types mostly,
who think it will always be chaos, that the world
will never be amenable to our reason
and to what we can do, what we are capable of.
It's not a world to be good in.
That's why I gave up thinking.
I'd rather be painting the kitchen.

Ah here he is at last
Philly in the front seat for once
and both of them waving like mad.
They must have something to tell me.

AN ENDING

So again I look out the window,
through the cobwebs, plant-pots and trees,
looking for something that will make
or start a poem, something significant
as I think it must be,
a thought at least, some cogitation
that will emerge perhaps from the nest out there,
not a commonplace
but something that will end a poem
surprisingly, satisfactorily.

IF YOU COULD READ THIS

i.m. my father

in your best pullover,
munro-spun tie,
seeking relaxation,

numbers in their
never-teetering columns
stood behind you

added up, impassive,
offering nothing
save security,

necessity,
no freedom

except from

the fate of
arts-wallahs,
trouser-behind

hanging out,
the fear for your son,
disappointment.

if you could read this
what difference
would it make?

THE COLLIER'S GRANDSON

i.m. Tony Harrison

Why does this picture sit on my wall
What is it first of all?
Having done some research
I can say it is a portrait
of 'the lily maid of Astolat'
that is Elaine whose hopeless love
of Lancelot is nowhere better shown
than here, carried in her fingertips
caressing the colours of his lustrous shield.
She is beautiful in her long, blue dress,
her blonde hair down to her waist
but gathered at her lovely nape.
She does not weep. She is alone.

It was my mother's picture
and stood a mystery before me
all the days of my childhood
which answers why it sits here now,
nostalgia, something to remember her by,
we must remember.

How my mother came by the picture
I can't say. Did it come with her
from home, perhaps acquired
by her mother? Certainly not her collier father
who had no use for idylls of any kind.
Then why a picture of this kind,
so resolutely Victorian,
the lure of the mediaeval,
the castle walls of certain stone,
embroidered cushions, sumptuous curtains.
It all seems to reach for gentility
as everything does that surrounds the maid,
alone in her tower-room, devoted
to the care of Lancelot's precious shield.
Not an image of noble but warlike Lancelot,
nor his king, nor adulterous Guinivere
is chosen for this special place,
but this modest, unsuccessful maid,
not as she was torn apart by tears
but here in the composure of her love.

So why is this picture kept on my wall?
Nostalgia as I have said– I *must* remember.
Or irony perhaps as this is nothing like
the other prints and pictures round about.
Old-fashioned it has always seemed,
sub-pre-Raphaelite, Tennysonian,

not my thing at all.
Perhaps I should have thrown it out.
It is only art, a genteel object
with no purchase on the growing boy.
Thrown into the bin it would find
its proper place for me, the collier's grandson,
trying hard not to be caught by art.
All this attends 'the lily maid of Astolat'.

ELEVEN-PLUS

The Book of Samuel, Ch XVI, 'Samuel anoints David'.
After a brief gloss of its meaning,
anoints is a word for the blackboard
and the weekly spelling test on one side
of folded foolscap, the other for mental arithmetic.
Who would come top this week?
The whole class ranked by desk,
twenty spellings and twenty sums.
Miss B – told us once
that if prideful human beings reached the moon
the Almighty would destroy the earth
which He had so graciously given to Mankind.
That would learn us.

NEAR CARDIFF

Let me recall a railway near Cardiff
where a train is stopped outside a station
and I am lifted by a soldier
to the ground. No one is alive now
to validate this story which even I
barely remember, the knickerbockered boy
lifted down in the pallid afternoon.
But these are the kind of moments
that fill a mind and make a life.

HOLLYBUSH

I know this is a dream,
so familiar, if not just here, Blurton Road,
walking towards the bus-stop
outside the selling-out place
where I think a friend's mother used to work.
Someone is already waiting.
Will the bus be long?
Behind me the road dips down
and then rises steeply to Hollybush
and the bus-stop nearest
to where my cousins used to live.
They are present to me now
only in half-dreams such as this.
The bus, when it comes,
will, I remember, be taking me
the other way.

NOTES

Hearts Desire

Thomas Müntzer: Among the several sources used in the writing of this poem, by far my greatest debt is to E. G. Rupp's fine and sensitive study of Müntzer in his book *Patterns of Reformation* (Epworth Press, 1969).

Both the *Five Winter Songs* and *Heart's Desire* include poems which have derived part of their verbal suggestion from earlier writing. None of them is in any sense a translation, or even an imitation, and frequently only one or two lines or phrases have been worked into my poems. Nonetheless they often provide the kindling for those poems, and so I think specific acknowledgement should be made. As will be seen their ready accessibility is often owed to a no more out of the way source than Penguin Books.

Five Winter Songs

Lope de Vega Carpio, 'Mañanicas floridas', *The Penguin Book of Spanish Verse,* ed. J. M. Cohen, p. 239.

Lope de Vega Carpio, 'Cantorcillo de la Virgen', ibid., p. 241.

'Whanne ic se on Rode', 14th Century English, *Medieval English Lyrics,* ed. R. T. Davies, (Faber), poem No. 30.

'Winter rouses all my grief', from the Harley Lyrics, translated by Brian Stone, *Medieval English Verse,* (Penguin), poem No. 76.

Heart's Desire

The poem used as an epigraph is included in *The Penguin Book of German Verse,* ed. Leonard Forster, p. 12.

'One Love Poem (after Lorca)': 'Es Verdad' ('It is True') translated by Harriet de Onis, *The Selected Poems of Federico Garcia*

Lorca, eds. Francisco Garcia Lorca and Donald M. Allen (New Directions), p. 41.

'The Day Comes': 'Entre moi et mon ami', an anonymous aube, 12th Century French, *The Penguin Book of French Verse* 1, ed. Brian Woledge, p. 88.

'The Fierce Dream':'Ich hab die Nacht geträumet', *The Penguin Book of German Verse,* p. 89.

'Despair (Desesperada)': the four lines quoted are from Wordsworth's 'Ode to Duty'.

The Red-Headed Pupil

Part One: The Anatomy Lesson

Rembrandt's *The Anatomy Lesson of Dr Nicholas Tulp*

'shows the master-surgeon surrounded by eager-eyed disciples, in the act of dissecting the left arm of a corpse. The apparent rendering of a real moment involved a good deal of artistic licence since dissection, at that time, started at the stomach, not the arm.'

The Anatomy Lesson of Dr Johan Deyman

'In this, the doctor's assistant holds the top of the skull inverted in his hand like a small basin while the doctor unravels the cadaver's brain. It hangs down on either side of the face like an old pullover. The viewer stares at the underside of the dead man's pale feet.' Adam Hopkins, *Holland, Its History, Paintings and People,* Faber & Faber, 1988, pp.69 & 80.

'What is needed is something we do not have: a theory of conscious organisms as physical systems composed of chemical elements and occupying space, which also have an individual perspective on the world, and in some cases the capacity for self-awareness as well.' Thomas Nagel, *The View from Nowhere,* Oxford University Press, 1986, p.51.

XII George B. Bridgman, *The Human Machine: The anatomical structure and mechanism of the human body,* 1938; Dover, New York, 1972.

XIII 'That supples...' Edward Young, citation in *Shorter Oxford English Dictionary* for *lubricate.*

XV & XVI 'this loam...' *Shakespeare, A Midsummer Night's Dream,* Act V, Sc i.

XVI '... the primary visual cortex (also known as the striate cortex or area 17), the most elementary of the cortical regions concerned with vision.' *The Brain: A Scientific American Book,* 1979, p.84.

XVIII 'First, Darwin argues that evolution has no purpose. Individuals struggle to increase the representation of their genes in future generations, and that is all...' Stephen Jay Gould, *Ever Since Darwin: Reflections in Natural History,* 1978; Pelican Books 1980, p.12.

XIX On 'The mollusc Nautilus... 'Richard Dawkins, *The Blind Watchmaker,* 1986; Penguin Books, 1988, pp.85-6.

XXI Bertrand de Born, in Dante, *Inferno,* Canto XXVIII, 1 121-3.

XXII 'Let man then contemplate the whole of nature in her full and grand majesty, and turn his vision from the low objects

which surround him.'
from Pascal, *Pensée 72,* trans. W.F. Trotter, Everyman, 1931.

XXIII Professor Eucalyptus said, "The search
For reality is as momentous as
The search for god."
from Wallace Stevens, 'An Ordinary Evening in New Haven', XXII, *Collected Poems,* Faber & Faber, 1955, p.481.

Part Two: Free Rein

'We cannot help acting under the idea of freedom, it seems; we are *stuck* deliberating as if our futures were open.'
Daniel C. Dennett, *Elbow Room, The Varieties of Free Will Worth Wanting,* Clarendon Press, Oxford, 1984, p.108.

I The people say that Cain slew Abel in the village of Zebdany ten miles to the north, and that for forty years he carried him on his back, not knowing what to do with him. On the slopes of this mountain he noticed a raven which was digging a hole to bury one of its kin; so he copied the bird and interred his own brother there.'
Colin Thubron, *Mirror to Damascus,* 1967; Century edition 1986, p.22.

IV Tom Williams, Guto, Dick Williams, Wil bach, Dafydd Dew
and me,
We are the people;'
from Emyr Humphreys, 'A Democratic Vista' XV *of Ancestor Worship,* Gwasg Gee, Denbigh, 1970.

V 'The poorest he that is in England has a life to live as the greatest he, and therefore ... every man that is to live under a government ought first by his own consent to put himself under that government.' Colonel Rainborough at the 'Putney Debates', 1647, as quoted in Christopher Hill, *The Century of Revolution, 1603-1714,* Thos Nelson, Edinburgh, 1961, pp.130-1.

VI 'Down that long dark lode ... he ... skated home'. Charles Kingsley, citation in *Shorter Oxford English Dictionary* for *lode.*

IX 'Immensity and emptiness: poverty and destitution. "I can lock my hunger in the coils of my entrails," writes an Arab poet, "as firmly as a skilful spinning-girl holds in her hand the threads her fingers twist." It was one of the companions of Muhammad, Abu Huraira, who said of the Prophet, "He went out of this world without once feasting on barley bread." Even in the heart of the richest countries, in Baghdad, how many poor men, like the humble folk in the *Thousand and One Nights,* have dreamed of a buttered cake made with white flour!' Fernand Braudel, *The Mediterranean and the Mediterranean World in the Age of Philip II,* Volume I, 1949, 1966; trans. Sian Reynolds, Fontana/Collins, London, 1975, p.173.

XI 'Who loves not home...' from W.J. Linton, 'Bob Thin, or The Poorhouse Fugitive' (1845), in Brian Maidment, *The Poorhouse Fugitives, Self-taught poets and poetry in Victorian Britain,* Carcanet, Manchester, 1987, p.80.

XXII 'If humans are seen as aspects of a process, they are seen as worked over by such massive mechanisms as natural selection, the process through which survival of traits is determined by the environment. The subjective viewpoints of creatures are of little interest and, in fact, raise the spectre of what evolutionists term the "teleological fallacy" (the fallacy that subjective purposes affect the evolutionary process, which, instead, should be seen as governed by the law of natural selection regardless of any petty motives and purposes of the creatures involved, including humans).' James L. Peacock, *The Anthropological Lens, Harsh Light, Soft Focus,* Cambridge University Press, 1986, pp.98-9.

XXIII 'We must turn our attention to the circumstances in which people act and by which they are formed, and we must change the question from "How should we live, whatever the circumstances?" to "Under what circumstances is it possible to live as we should?"' Thomas Nagel, *Equality and Partiality,* Oxford University Press, 1991, p.52.

<u>The Weak Spot</u>

'For the moment perhaps I was Frazer and she was confirming that no matter what complication, injury, foulness, she didn't back down from her belief that all rested on the gentleness in privacy of man and woman — they did in willing desire what in the rock and water universe, die green universe, the bestial universe, was done from ignorant necessity.'
Saul Bellow, *The Adventures of Augie March,* 1953; Penguin edition, 1966, p.317.

Clarity or Death!

The following notes acknowledge the sources of direct and adapted quotations that appear in the poems or their titles.

we may be able to reduce the number of different things: Richard P. Feynman, *Six Easy Pieces, The Fundamentals of Physics Explained,* 1998.

the visible universe can only be of the kind that permits us: John D. Barrow, *The Origin of the Universe*, London, 1994.

the starting state of the universe must have been very highly ordered: Barrow, as above.

the universe is like a pool that has had a stone thrown into it: Attributed to Origen (c.185–c.254).

all the ordered forms of energy in the universe… : Barrow, as above.

there may be symmetrical universes but they are not ours: Ian Stewart, *Nature's Numbers, Discovering Order and Pattern in the Universe*, 1995.

musicians wrestle everywhere: after Emily Dickinson.

'against those who refuse definitions': see Aristotle, *Metaphysics*, Book IV, 4.

what need we know of the workings of Nature… : Roger Penrose, *The Emperor's New Mind, Concerning Computers, Minds, and the Laws of Physics*, 1990.

faith in reason is the trust that… : A.N. Whitehead, *Science and the Modern World*, 1925.

… *and with the Indian figures 987654321 and zephira …*: see George Ifrah, *The Universal History of Numbers from Prehistory to the Invention of the Computer*, trans. Bellos, Harding, Wood and Monk, 1998.

a real sum is a sum of real people: after the title of a photo sequence by Mario Merz.

the wall that separates ...: from José Saramago, *The Year of the Death of Ricardo Reis*, trans. Giovanni Pontiero, 1991.

'Mere Bagatelle'

Epigraph: ... sometimes out of the corner of an eye... : Jerry Fodor on Richard Dawkins, *London Review of Books*, 18 April 1996.

set yourself steadily... : John Ruskin, *The Elements of Drawing*, 1857.

vast Rondures: after Walt Whitman, 'Passage to India', Chant V, 1871.

15. *of cousinhood or uncleship* – and *for a brief while*: after Charles Lamb, 'The Wedding', *Elia and The Last Essays of Elia*, 1835.

18. *vous avez perdu l'homme il faudra le retrouver ce ne sera pas facile*: Victor Serge, *Les années sans pardon*, 1971.

26. *God's inordinate fondness for beetles:* A 'quip' attributed to the biologist J.B.S. Haldane.

p. 167 31. *the figure raising his arm in the main boat...* : after James Hamilton on J.M.W. Turner's *'Now for the Painter'* in *Turner, The Late Seascapes*, 2003.

p. 169 34. *Cain says: there is no judgement and no judge...* : *Targum Pseudo-Jonathan* to *Genesis*, 4, 1–8 quoted in *The Oxford Bible Commenatary*, 2001.

p. 173 38. *For thee...* : After John Dryden, 'Lucretius, The beginning of the First Book', 1685.
How EXQUISITELY... : after William Wordsworth, 'Prospectus' to *The Excursion*, 1814.

The sunbeam said, 'Be happy.': Wordsworth, *The Recluse*, Part First, Book First, 1806.

The Reasoner

The following notes acknowledge the sources of direct or adapted quotations that appear in the poems.

1 'History could make a stone weep', Marilynne Robinson, *Gilead* (2004), p 216. 'Human beings do not make history … Rather it is history that makes human beings and thereby absolves them from blame', Fernand Braudel, *A History of Civilisations*, quoted by Albert Manguel, review in the *Independent*, 6 March 1994.

5–9 'Is our language complete?': '… ask yourself whether our language is complete', Ludwig Wittgenstein, *Philosophical Investigations*, trans. G.E.M. Anscombe (1953; 2001), no. 18.

30 'me own ataraxy'; after *ataraxia*: state of tranquillity free of all disturbance, as achieved by Epicurean philosophy; Samuel Beckett, *Molloy* (1979), p. 40: '… I grew calm again and was restored, in the face of nature's pranks, to my old ataraxy, for what it was worth.'

45–46 After two paintings by the Australian artist James Gleeson (1915–2008).

52 'the nature and foundation of government …': David Hume, *A Treatise of Human Nature* (1739), Book I, 'Of the Understanding', section VII.

53 After some of the prints in the series *Miserere* by Georges Rouault (1871–1958).

54 'Inasmuch as life …': 'To talk of intrinsic right and wrong is absolutely nonsensical: intrinsically, an injury, an oppression, an exploitation, an annihilation can be nothing wrong, in as much as life is *essentially* … something which functions by injuring, oppressing, exploiting, and annihilating, and is absolutely incomprehensible without such a character', Friedrich Nietzsche, *The Genealogy of Morals* (1887), quoted by Philippa Foot, *Natural Goodness* (2001), p. 110.

ACKNOWLEDGEMENTS

Hearts Desire
Many of these poems first appeared in *Stand*, and I should like to express my particular appreciation of that magazine and my thanks to its editors for their continuing interest and encouragement.

A number of the poems in the first part of the book were collected in *The Important Man* (Northern House, 1970).

Acknowledgement and thanks are also due to *Agenda*, *The 42nd Street Trip* (Brooklyn, New York), *Iowa Review* and *North West Arts News* where some of the poems also first appeared, and to the editors of *Michigan Quarterly Review* (IX, 3), *New Poems 1973-4*, *Poetry of the Committed Individual*, and *Poetry Introduction 3* (Faber) for reprinting various poems.

Above all my thanks are due to Judith Wainwright, for her constant help, and for the care and the acuteness of her criticism.

Selected Poems

This collection contains poems that have previously been published in *The Important Man* (Northern House, 1970), and *Heart's Desire* (Carcanet, 1978).

Further acknowledgement and thanks are due as follows: for 'Transitive' to *Stand;* for 'Sea Dreams' to *Poetry Supplement* for the Poetry Book Society, Christmas 1981, reprinted in *Helix* (Australia) and *The Agni Review* (US); for 'The Mad Talk of George III and A Hymn to Liberty' to *Poetry Now* (BBC Radio 3), and *Poetry Nation Review*, reprinted *Harvard Magazine* (US) and *Some Contemporary Poets of Britain and Ireland.*

I should like to thank the Department of English and History in the Faculty of Humanities of Manchester Polytechnic for the leave during which this book was completed.

The Red- Headed Pupil

The Anatomy Lesson' appeared under the title The Red-Headed Pupil' in *PN Review* 80, July-August 1991.

An earlier version of 'The Weak Spot' appeared in *The Flying Pig*, Department of English and History, The Manchester Metropolitan University, Autumn 1991.

'Free Rein', no XXI, under the tide of 'Cause and...' the *Independent* 3rd February 1994.

The Judith E. Wilson Fund, the Faculty of English and St John's College, University of Cambridge, for a Visiting Fellowship in Autumn 1985.

The Head of Department and colleagues in English and History at The Manchester Metropolitan University for sabbatical and personal support.

To Mike Fuller, Elspeth Graham, Avril Horner, Alf Louvre and Brian Maidment who have given me advice and encouragement at important times, and special thanks to Michael Schmidt and Judith Wainwright.

Out of Air

'Out of the Air' appeared first in the *Times Literary Supplement*, 9 August 1996.

'The Apparent Colonnades' was broadcast on BBC Radio 3 in 1996 and published in *PN Review* 115, 1997.

'Anne's Shells' has appeared in *Grand Street*, New York.

Thanks for reading, advice and support to Jon Glover, Avril Horner, and to the Department of English at The Manchester Metropolitan University. Especial thanks to Michael Schmidt and Judith Wainwright.

'Broken Symmetry', '... that the whole universe ... etc', Paul Claudel in *The Correspondence 1899–1926 between Paul Claudel and André Gide*, trans John Russell, London: Secker & Warburg, 1952, pp. 53-4.

'Form Law Order Sequence' draws upon Henry Adams (1838-1918), specifically *The Education of Henry Adams* (1907; 1918), Ch XV, 'Darwinism'.

'The Humane House' draws upon Henry David Thoreau (1817-62), specifically 'The Beach', Ch IV, and 'The Sea and the Desert', Ch IX of *Cape Cod*, Thomas Y. Crowell, New York, 1961, Apollo edition, New York, 1966. The epigraph is from his *Walden, or Life in the Woods* (1854), 'Economy', Holt Rinehart and Winston, New York, 1963, p.18.

'The Apparent Colonnades' takes its title from a painting by Michael Andrews in The Whitworth Art Gallery, Manchester.

' "War Poems": Six Pieces', 'The dead are unhappy enough . . . etc', Marguerite Long, pianist and widow of Captain Joseph de Marliave, who gave the first performance of Maurice Ravel's *Le Tombeau de Couperin*, a work dedicated to her first husband and five other friends of Ravel killed in the 1914-18 War. Quoted in Gerald Larner, *Maurice Ravel*, London: Phaidon, 1966, p.164.

Clarity or Death

Special thanks to Judith Wainwright and Jon Glover, to my patient publisher Michael Schmidt, Judith Willson and all at Carcanet. Thanks too to a group of MA students from Manchester Metropolitan University for their comments on '... *and with the Indian figures 987654321 and zephira* ...'.

Some of these poems have appeared in *Cincinnati Review*, *Moving Worlds*, *PN Review*, *Stand*, and *The Reader*.

The Reasoner

Special thanks for discussion and encouragement to Judith Wainwright, Shirley Chew, Jon Glover, Rachel Mann, John McAuliffe, Helen Tookey, John Whale; to Michael Schmidt, Judith Willson, Eleanor Crawforth and all at Carcanet; to Leonid Lerman for his generous permission for use of the cover image, and to Elizabeth Cook and Helen Tookey for permission to use quotations in the epigraphs.

Several parts of *The Reasoner* have previously appeared elsewhere under different titles. I am grateful to the editors of the following publications:

American Poetry Review; *Eyewear* (toddswift.blogspot.com); *The Manchester Review* (www.the manchesterreview.co.uk); *Moving*

Worlds; *The North*; *PN Review*; *Poetry & Audience*; *Revista Canarias de Estudios Ingleses*, no. 60, 2010 (Universidad de La Laguna); *Revue LISA / LISA e-journal* (Littératures, histoires des Idées, Sociétés du monde Anglophone), vol. 7, no. 3, 2009, Festschrift honouring René Gallet (www.lisa.revues.org/72); *Stand*; *The Wolf.*

What Must Happen
Thanks are due to the editors of the following publications, in which some of these poems first appeared: *Times Literary Supplement*, *PN Review*, *Poetry and Audience*, *Stand*, and *The Warwick Review.*

As Best We Can
Some of these poems have appeared in *PN Review*, *Stand* and the *Times Literary Supplement*. Thanks for criticism and encouragement to my indefatigable editor Michael Schmidt and all at Carcanet and to Jon Glover, Robert Gray, J.J. Healy, John Lancaster, Alf Louvre, John McAuliffe, Judith Wainwright and John Whale.
Here on Earth
Some of these poems have appeared in *The Manchester Review, Moving Worlds, PN Review, Poetry and Audience, Raceme, Stand,* and in an on-line poetry anthology at Manchester Metropolitan University.

Many thanks for criticism and encouragement to my editors Michael Schmidt and John McAuliffe and to all at Carcanet as well as Jon Glover, Robert Gray, J.J. Healy, Alf Louvre, Judith Wainwright and John Whale.

'Here on Earth' is dedicated to the memory of my friend Adolfo Trippini.